Towards Better Practices in Distance Education

Towards Better Practices in Distance Education

Dr. M. V. Lakshmi Reddy
MA, MEd, PhD, PGDIS, PGDDE, LLB, CIC

KANISHKA PUBLISHERS, DISTRIBUTORS
NEW DELHI-110 002

KANISHKA PUBLISHERS, DISTRIBUTORS
4697/5-21A, Ansari Road, Daryaganj
New Delhi-110 002.
Phones : 327 0497, 328 8285
Fax : 011-328 8285

First Published 2001

ISBN 81-7391-445-1

PRINTED IN INDIA

Published by Madan Sachdeva for Kanishka Publishers, Distributors, 4697/5-21A, Ansari Road, Daryaganj, New Delhi-110 002; Typeset by Arora Computer Point, Delhi, and Printed at Nice Printing Press, Delhi.

Foreword

I am glad that Dr. M.V. Lakshmi Reddy has raised certain issues which should have been addressed long ago by those who profess to care for standards, quality and commitment in the filed of education in general and distance education in particular. It is not uncommon in the developing and, to some extent the developed countries, too, to mix up professionalism with clever opportunism; and institutional commitment with struggle for survival, no matter how all these are actually killing the very core of professionalism and the institutional images. Liberalisation and market forces have only accelerated this unethical and anti-social process by legitimizing spurious and often nefarious activities of individuals and powerful coteries operating under the cover of educational banners. Often, the top managements either look the other way or actively promote such activities in various forms. Little they realize that unless basic minimum standards with regard to professional competence of individuals as well as the institutions are insisted upon, the whole edifice of educational superstructure would crumble with the slightest jolt.

In the context of distance education, the dangers confronting teaching as profession are daunting. The risks staring at the innocent learners who, for want of alternatives, enroll in thousands for any distance education course offered by any institution, are equally enormous. Inconsistence and dubious professionalism will spoil the system as a whole, if they are not tackled tactfully and urgently. Unless the top managements are sensitive, serious and caring, institutions and individuals will not meet the minimum standards automatically, notwithstanding the clamour for academic freedom and the rest of the opportunistic slogans. After all, individuals make the institutions, and if the institutions do not care for competence, commitment and academic excellence, both institutions and individuals working in them will fall into disrepute. It is in this context the issues related to professionalism acquire importance.

Distance Open Learning (DOL) has already become a reality of the present. Indications are that DOL has spread much more rapidly than was expected. The very spread of DOL throws up numerous challenges in terms of services to learners and quality of their learning. Non-serious approaches to meeting the commitments made would cost the system dearly, although some vested interests may be flourishing precisely because of the non-serious approach of institutions. Here, too, professionalism and commitment of individuals and top managements would matter. The present book discusses a number of issues in some detail. One may disagree with the manner in which the issues have been dealt with but none can brush them aside as unimportant or irrelevant. To ignore them anymore would be promoting non-professionalism in the name of promoting education and distance education. I wish Dr. Reddy all success in his endeavour.

New Delhi

Prof. P.R. Ramanujam
Director
Staff Training and Research Institute
in Distance Education
Indira Gandhi National Open University
Maidan Garhi, New Delhi-110068

Preface

Establishment of Open Universities has heralded a new era in the history of distance and open education. There are about 40 Open Universities in the world out of which 10 (25%) are located in India alone. As regards the Distance and Open Education Institutions, the number is around 1200 spread over 120 countries of which 72 (6%) are in India alone. As a sequel to this magnitude of growth, many Associations of Open and Distance Education/Learning have grown at national, regional and international level. To name a few such Associations: Indian Distance Education Association (IDEA), Australian Association for Open and Distance Learning (AAODL), Asian Association of Open Universities (AAOU), International Council for Distance and Open Education (ICDOE) and so on. These Open and Distance Education Universities/Institutes and professional bodies have established a wide network at national, regional and international level. This network, in the process, has brought hundreds of thousands of teachers, academics and other personnel involved in distance education into it and they have been interacting amongst themselves at different levels.

These Associations or Bodies have been striving hard to propagate, promote and strengthen distance and open learning at national and international level. These institutions and Associations at different levels have been playing significant role, both independently and collectively, in promoting, propagating and publicizing distance education through conferences, seminars, professional journals, sharing of their materials, etc. I, being part of distance education system, have been trying to reflect on the practice of distance education. As a part of this endeavour I could participate, whenever and wherever possible, at national and international conferences, seminars, and other such forums. Also, I could contribute, over a period, to different professional journals in distance and open education or learning . I am grateful to the relevant organizing committees of the Conferences, Seminars and other academic forums for accepting my papers and including the same in their respective reports. I am equally grateful to the appropriate committees and Boards of relevant journals for accepting and publishing my articles. This book is rather a collection of revised, reviewed and improved versions of these articles and papers which have been organized into different chapters under relevant themes. They have also been reasonably updated in view of the subsequent developments in the field. To be more specific, the details of chronology of these papers and articles which have been originally published in different forms are as follows:

(i) "A Scientific Approach to Organising Counselling for Distance Learners" in *Kakatiya Journal of Open Learning*, Vol. 2, No. 2, December, 1996.

(ii) "Action and Feedback Research in Distance Education: Some Priority Areas", a paper presented at *Professor G. Ram Reddy Memorial Seminar on Research in Distance Education in India*, November, 1996.

(iii) "Quantity and Quality of Distance Education: Some Issues of Student Support Services", a paper accepted and submitted to the *11th Annual Conference of Asian Association of Open Universities*, November, 1997.

(iv) "Towards a Consortium for Distance Education in India: Issues and Problems", a paper presented at the *International Conference on Collaborative and Networked Learning,* organized by IGNOU in February, 1998.

(v) A book review (An Investigative Review of a plagiarized book on distance education) in *Journal of Educational Planning and Administration*, Vol. XII, No. 2, April, 1998.

(vi) "Dropout Problem: An Overview", a paper presented at *VI Annual Conference of Indian Distance Education Association (IDEA)*, held at Nasik in January, 1999.

(vii) "The Future of Distance Education and Distance Education of the Future", a paper accepted at the *International Conference of International Council for Distance and Open Education*, held in Austria in June, 1999.

(viii) "Teachers and (other) Academics in IGNOU: A Retrospect and Prospect" in *Journal of Distance Education*, Vol. 6, No. 7, 1999.

(ix) "Changing Academics and Emerging Professionalism: How to Reform?" in *University News*, Vol. 38, No. 25, 2000.

(x) "Defining the Unreached through Distance and Open Learning: A Typological Perspective", a paper presented at the *IDEA Conference* held at New Delhi in April, 2000.

As stated above, these articles and papers have been improved, updated and organized into different Chapters in this book. The book will be useful to the distance and open education teachers, academics, practitioners, researchers and all others interested in the field who have commitment to promotion of quality works or contributions by themselves and their peers or contemporaries in and outside the countries of their origin. It is equally useful to the distance learners, both hitherto reached and unreached through distance and open education. Any suggestions, comments or views on this book or any part of it are welcome and an attempt will be made to incorporate them in the successive edition.

M.V. Lakshmi Reddy

Contents

1

Introduction

Introduction

Quality of contributions of an educational institution can be attributed, directly or indirectly, to the quality of its teachers and academics. Distance and Open Education Institutions or Universities are no exception to it. In other words, quality of academic output of individual teachers and academics of an academic institution as a whole is dependent on their professional nature, quality and character. In addition to this, the status of these teachers and academics in terms of their designation, process of selection, terms and conditions of services including the privileges, if any attached, will have a significant bearing on the quality and character of their contribution. Of course, the contributions of all teachers and academics of any particular institutions cannot have uniform quality or standards. As the individual differences are bound to exist, as far as the competence is concerned, the quality of products of these academics cannot also be uniform. In majority of these institutions in a country like India, only a few of the teachers and academics are really committed to the institution and are really competent to contribute to their respective disciplines or fields, be it teaching, research and/or extension.

In other words, the majority of them, in general, are mediocre without any commitment either to the profession or to the institution, but with full of manipulative skills including high degree of sycophancy, hypocrisy, etc. In fact, these manipulations have been fetching them highly satisfying results from the top brass of the institution which has unfortunately been equally susceptible to such manipulations. This must be so not only in India but also in many developing countries, and even in a few so called developed countries. In such state-of-the-art situation it will be too much to expect high quality products from such mediocre, majority community who are ruling the roost of the higher education institutions in general and distance education institutions/universities in particular.

As a result of the above, perhaps, the status of teachers and academics in these institutions, has also undergone a change. Their professionalism and the nature and quality of their products varied significantly from individual to individual in an institution, and from institution to institution in a country or across the countries. Of course, one cannot draw any generalisations by taking into account the situation of any one particular individual teacher or academic or an institution. However, a national institution or University in any country can be taken as a representative one of the particular country and can be used as an example to infer something from it regarding the quality of its (the country's) teachers and academics. Moreover, if such national institution/ university is one among the internationally accredited or acknowledged institutions that can be taken as a perfect example or case and truly representative one.

It was interesting to hear to and also read through some of the writings in distance and open education by the pioneers of it in certain countries spread over different continents. They were, of course, popular not only in the respective countries of their origin but also at international level. From the above experiences I could identify three major or broad objectives of distance and open education in any country. They include:

(a) addressing the growing educational needs, problems and demands of the population which the conventional institutions have failed to address adequately;

(b) democratisation of education by enhancing educational access and opportunities to all the needy sections of population through flexible, massive and cost-effective multimedia education;

(c) promotion of quality education by minimising differentials in offering education and by subjecting teaching to public audit; and

(c) gradual institutionalisation of distance and open education at all levels of education to promote continuing and lifelong education of all people of the society as a whole.

But, the quality of teachers and other academics in distance education institutions, amongst others, determines the realisation of these objectives in the respective countries. In view of this, the cynical and mediocre teachers and academics in these institutions should be identified and their dangerous, unhealthy and perverted designs and practices to subvert the system from within should be defeated before they succeed in defeating the purpose of distance education itself.

In order to succeed in this endeavour, the instructional materials and publications, in whatever the quality they are available, of the distance teachers and academics, should be thoroughly reached to their colleagues, peers and contemporaries at different places in different institutions on one hand, and to the distance learners as well as to the public on the other for timely and appropriate academic audit. It is in this context, the author endeavours to make the distance teachers and academics understand the quality of their contemporaries elsewhere and at the same time to reach the unreached learners through the existing programmes and courses that are on offer. This book is precisely an attempt in this direction and is presented under three sections and ten chapters in all.

Chapter 1, in fact, presents the summary of different sections and chapters included in this book. Section -I touches upon the changing status of teachers and academics in India in general and in distance education in particular and their professionalism, including plagiarism. It also exemplifies such status and professionalism through selected academic works and institutions. Chapter 2 throws light on the changing nature of academics and their emerging professionalism, with a focus on plagiarism. This chapter provides an insight into different types and degrees of plagiarism, professional manipulations and reproductions resorted to by the teachers and academics. Chapter 3 presents the prospects and retrospect of teachers and (other) academics in distance and open learning institutions in India with special reference to the Indira Gandhi National Open University (IGNOU). Also, it touches upon the nature, quality and role of academic administration that has been confused in taking decisions regarding staffing of teachers and other academics. This section, thus, presents the emerging status and professionalism of teachers and (other) academics in general and in distance and open education in India in particular.

Distance and open education institutions have been taking pride in the increasing enrolment of their students year by year. But, they have been ignoring or paying less attention to the problem of dropouts among their students. Like in conventional system, the problem of dropout in distance and open education has been a major cause of wastage. In addition, if these dropouts share their nightmarish experiences with the potential learners, they would be thoroughly discouraged from enrolling for any programme of study of these institutions. This would eventually cause a disastrous to the very survival of distance and open education system itself. It calls for systematic efforts to address all the problems, barriers, etc. related to the programme of learners and thereby to arrest and reduce the rate of dropout. In order to reduce the dropout rate of students there should therefore be qualitative and quantitative improvement in delivery of distance education programmes. The reduction in dropout is just not possible through mere expansion of delivery network of regional, study, programme and work centers and partner institutions, amongst others. Of course, there have been efforts to bring into this network the different institutions with diverse nature and potential so as to add variety and diversity to the network. But, to facilitate effective utilisation of the support services of this network by the students there should be a systematic counselling organised for them on scientific basis. Also, there is a need for serious feedback and action research on the fast expanding and diverse delivery network to address various problems arising out of it. Only then the expansion of the system will be meaningful and the delivery of programmes will be effective and efficient. Section-II focuses on all these aspects of distance education, Chapter 4 specifically discusses the nature, types, time/points of dropout among distance learners and the reasons for their dropout as well. It presents rather an overview of global situation of dropout touching upon these aspects. Chapter 5 is devoted to identification of qualitative and quantitative aspects and issues of programme delivery that require thorough consideration at different stages of development of the programmes. Chapter 6 attempts to present scientific approach to organising counselling for distance learners with a view to effectively addressing their real problems felt needs, grievances, barriers, etc. in pursing their programmes, Chapter 7 highlights the need for conducting feedback and action research into distance education and identifies the priority areas thereof and the issues involved in so doing.

Section III, containing three chapters (Chapters 8-10), is a special focus on maximising the reach with a view to reaching the hitherto unreached people and the places. It is an undisputed fact that the failure of the conventional system in addressing the expanding and diversified educational needs, problems and demands of different sections of the society has led to the origin and growing importance of non-formal education system. Distance and Open Education as an innovation in non-formal education has now become a universally accepted practice and has established itself as an effective alternative to the conventional system, besides supplementing and complementing it. The future of distance and open education has, thus been, changing with its growing prospects and increasing functions in the dynamic global society. Added to this, the unabated advancements in information and communication technology (ICT) have metamorphosed the nature and character of distance education. Its generational changes from print mode through virtual on-line mode are in fact the outcomes of these advancements only. Now one can notice increasing growth and rapid emergence of virtual campuses or universities, which are really without any walls. With this kind of future of distance education, distance education of the future can be very much different. It will be an era of virtual campuses wherein the students will be able to have access to not one, but to many such campuses at a time right from their homes. For this they should, of course, be able to own or should be enabled to have access to a computer with internet facility at their homes or other places. Also, they should be enabled to get all the support services related to their programmes of study mostly at their homes itself. At the same time, given the differential in the economic status of the countries across the globe there will not also be any dearth of distance education institutions which will still be toiling with or struggling hard to deliver even the printed materials to their students by post. Thus, there will be circles or layers of distance education institutions with top layer encompassing virtual universities, other layers or circles will be having in them the distance education institutions that fall under different lower generations at global level. Chapter 8 deals with all these aspects of distance education vis-à-vis developed, developing and underdeveloped countries of the world. Nevertheless, whatever the efforts are put by the distance education institutions (by exploiting all available and affordable ICT) to enhance access to education, to democratize education and to offer quality education to all, it will be very difficult to promote equality in the above respects.

Further, the fact that the physical, social, cultural, economic, educational and technological conditions of the individual learners can never be equal and thus can never be ignored. Hence, there will always be groups of enrolled learners and the potential learners with different (dis)abilities who are inadequately or differently reached or who remain to be reached in one sense or the other. Therefore, it is essential to define and identify different types of learners unreached through distance and open learning. Such an effort would help in formulating appropriate strategies which can enhance access to quality education and opportunities for democratisation of education. Chapter 9 is an attempt in this direction.

ICT has made it possible for any learner to pursue education from any place and from any institution. Yet, the learner's geographical mobility from place to place, be it within a country or across the countries, has been causing problems to him in pursuing his programme of study, depending upon the nature, duration, etc. of the programme. To address all these problems, there is a need for effective network of distance and open education institutions with provisions for transfer of students along with their credits, records, and so on between and/or among all the institutions offering same programmes, in same media, with same or equivalent syllabus or curriculum. Such a network calls for a well coordinated mechanism to smoothen and facilitate the relevant operations. If this kind of transfer is made possible through different media, including the virtual mode that will be the best every day for the distance learners at large. This, perhaps, is possible by promoting multiple consortia at different levels—national, regional and international - and through multiple media. The last chapter discusses the need and scope of multiple consortia, along with relevant problems and issues, particularly in a multilingual country like India. Of course, these problems and issues related to multiple consortia in India will hold equally good to the consortia at regional and global level. Such consortia will be the boons to the distance learners in this era of globalisation and liberalisation.

Section - I

Plagiarism and Changing Professionalism of Academics

2

Changing Academics and Emerging Professionalism: How to Reform?

Institutes of higher education, particularly Universities, are supposed to be the centres of excellence and the ivory towers of knowledge. But, to be honest and frank, the things have changed over time and are still changing to be otherwise. This is mainly because of the changed and still changing nature, quality and character of the academics—the teachers, researchers and others—of these institutes or Universities. Why did they change so? There can be many reasons that may include social, political, economic, cultural conditions and personality of these academics. The main purpose of this Chapter is, however, not to continue the discussion on the reasons therefor, but on the types of the academics, the nature and character of the emerging professionalism and the ways of reforming it.

The academics, in the Indian context, can be classified into three broad categories. They are:

1. the professionally committed and excelling academics, but a minority in terms of their number;
2. the professionally committed academics, but relatively less competent than the first category, and moderate in number; and

3. the professionally non-committed, incompetent and manipulative academics, but a majority in their number.

The professionalism fostered by the first category above is globally acknowledged, as it adheres to and maintains international standards, whatever they be. The academics of the second category strive towards acknowledged or acceptable professional practices. The third category of academics resort to the professionalism which is increasingly condemned, but unfortunately it has been emerging unchecked till date for want of appropriate and effective measures. What are the consequences of such a situation?

Many of us must have heard of a popular maxim "Right man for the right job". It is equally applicable to all jobs, whether big or small at familial, institutional, political, societal or global level. Goel and Goel (1999, p. 10) elaborate the maxim thus: "if we put a good man in a bad set up, he will make the things go through, while if we put a bad man in a good set up, he will make a mess of the whole situation." Here 'man' includes the 'woman' as well.

When it comes to an institution, it is not one man who makes or mars the things. It is often more than one—a group of people called "staff" that includes all from top to bottom—who share responsibility of good or bad performance in an institution or organisation. Walter R. Sharp (1961, p. 119) says: "even a poorly devised machinery may be made to work, if it is manned with well trained, intelligent, imaginative and devoted staff. On the other hand, the best planned organisation may produce unsatisfactory results, if it is operated by mediocre and disgruntled people". But, in the context of institutions such as universities and other academic institutions, what can one do to make the 'man' and the 'woman' work properly? Let us start from the top.

Vice-Chancellors

In the context of Indian Universities, Sarup (1999, p. 2) sums up the existing position of Vice-Chancellors thus:

> "It would be in bad taste to discuss what people have to do to become Vice-chancellors and what kind of compromises they have to make to stay on in the job. Suffice it to state that the common perception is that those who really deserve to be Vice-chancellors avoid it like the plague while the sycophants who get it by hook or by crook end up making a hash of Universities."

Since I do not know what exactly they do and what compromises they make, I cannot join this issue. However, there are vice-chancellors, the existing and the former, who are the right people to agree or disagree with or comment on what Sarup says. If the position of Vice-chancellors is really like what Sarup says, I cannot resist my temptation to pose an important question here.

Is sycophancy applicable only to those who have got or aspire to get the post of Vice-chancellor? Is it not equally applicable to academics? I think it is equally applicable to a vast majority of the academics who aspire for any higher post(s), academic or non-academic, in the universities.

Academics and Emerging Professionalism

Singh (1996, p. 6) describes the situation of academics in higher education system as follows:

> "It is unfortunate in the last twenty-five years or so, the 'mediocre' with no professionalism or commitment to the cause of higher education have dominated the scene and sought more 'freedom' to promote their narrow self-interests. They have been in the forefront, resisting every positive move for a change and surviving by ad-hocism or by spoiling work culture, wherever it existed. They have not only made education a burden to the exchequer but also a cause of social tension, thanks to their non-productive teaching and research".

As part of the higher education system the distance education institutions do not look any different. This is clear from what Ramanujam (1995, pp. 7-8) says:

> "Lack of critical and realistic approach breeds a strange variety of intellectuals who, with mediocre talents or at times none at all, manage to sneak into distance education institutions, capture by hook or by crook key positions and subvert the system from within. These parasites have the knack of convincing others about the advantages of the system without having conviction in themselves...... They master the art of sloganeering and sycophancy for the public consumption, and indulge in avoiding all hard work and challenges facing the system".

Being an academic I certainly do not have any hesitation in continuing the issue or debate on academics and their professionalism of the day.

I had already joined the issue in another context, and said:

> "In the academic world, competency breeds competency and the incompetent breed incompetent. While the minority competent academics are committed to strive towards excellence in their profession through fair means, the incompetent lot are committed to practise only manipulations as effective means to excel the competent and also to meet their professional and career ends. They find sheer manipulations as promising means to achieve their ends as the good academic credentials do for the competent" (Lakshmi Reddy, 1999).

At this point, it is important for me to mention that there is no dearth of academics who come out with publications full of verbatim reproductions with or without implicit or explicit acknowledgements, and plagiarism ranging from paragraphs to pages or entire documents, without any reference to the original source(s) or the author(s). Ambirajan (1998) exposes plagiarism, in course materials of an academic institution. Lakshmi Reddy (1998) provides ample evidence for plagiarism of different kinds and magnitude through an investigative review of a book on distance education. The following summary paragraph of the review of the book reflects the extent of plagiarism resorted to by the authors of that book on distance education:

> "While reading the book, the reviewer recalled to have read the same content ditto in some of the popular publications or documents of IGNOU, among other things. When the relevant publications or documents were revisited by the reviewer, startling facts started coming to light. The reviewer could find ditto verbatim reproductions and plagiarisations ranging from paragraphs to pages; without any reference to the original source or authors. To cite only a few instances: The authors have reproduced verbatim on pp.8-10 from Rumble (1989:28-36), on pp.116-118 from RSD (1992:7-10), on pp.152-155 from Khurana et al (1993:182-187), on p.51 (second and third paras) from Asha (1995:50), on p.110 (second para) from DDE (1989:32), on p.111 (first and fourth paras) from RSD (1989:12-13), on p.123 (second para) from Prasad (1992:16), on p.166 (last para) from DDE (1994:21), on p.172 (second para) from Gao (1991:55), on p.219 (fifth para) from Gentai et al (1993:p.27), on p.231 (second and fifth paras) from SOE (1992:28, 45-46), and so on. While the authors have not hesitated to reproduce verbatim a few pages from the publications of the University (IGNOU) and its faculty, it is needless to search for other texts reproduced. But if one has time to thoroughly scrutinise and investigate into the other sources, it is not difficult to prove that more than 95 per cent of the content of the book is nothing but plagiarism and the rest verbatim reproduction from the works already published. It is an irony that the foreword to such a book was written by a person no less than the Vice-chancellor of the National Open University of India." (ibid, pp. 231-232).

There are academics of another category who proliferate the academic work, of course, of their own. These academics present papers in national and international conferences, seminars, etc. They also get the same papers published in different forms such as an article in a journal or a chapter in a book. Of course, this is the most common and accepted practice both at national and international level. To cite just as examples are: Lakshmi Reddy (1996a, 1996b); Mohan Rao and Lakshmi Reddy (1992, 1996); Brahmaji Rao (1994a, 1994b). These are only few examples. If one has to quote such works exhaustively it will run into volumes.

There are some academics who proliferate their work by including the same chapter in different books without any indication or reference to the first publication at all. For example, Bakhshish Singh (1994, 1995); Brahmaji Rao (1994a, 1994b); Takwale (1994, 1995); Kamala (1994, 1995); Raja Mouli (1994, 1995); Prasad (1994, 1995); Subba Rao (1994, 1995); One can notice even the same editor concurrently editing different journals. For example, Panda (1997a, 1998a, 1999a); and Panda (1997b, 1998b, 1999b, 2000);

Further, one can, perhaps, identify such practices as the presentation of the same paper in different conferences / seminars; publication of the same article / review in different journals or periodicals; becoming an editor of journal(s) without having contributed to any article, research paper or review of any professional journal; becoming an editor of a book without having authored any book or without having contributed to any chapter to a book edited by others or even by himself or herself; ransacking of official / team work for personal publications; publication of an issue or two of a journal containing only conference / seminar papers (of course, already published as reports), and so on.

In addition to the above, one can also notice certain other practices followed by the changing academics to promnote their own carrier and of their clique. They include:

- Inclusion of same expert / professional in different selection committees / boards of different academic disciplines;
- Inclusion of more than one expert / professional from an outside institute / organisation on a selection committee / board;
- Informal mutual agreement(s) among the experts for mutual inclusion on selection committee(s) for

positions at certain levels in different institutions without hesitation;

- Careful exclusion / non-inclusion of competent professionals on selection and other committees / boards to push certain hidden agenda;
- Exclusion of competent / qualified candidates from competition for any academic position through manipulation; and
- Selection of candidates with irrelevant academic qualifications, credentials and experience for a position with a view to fraudulently suppressing the competent candidates with relevant qualifications, credentials and experience.

The emerging professionalism of the changing academics is, thus, full of manipulations and can be summarised as shown in Figure 2.1.

Nevertheless, are such practices applicable to only those academics or non-academics who are aspiring or occupying higher posts only? Of course, the above practices in different forms are seen in majority of the aspirants to and even occupants of all posts in the entire education system.

Pylee (1995, pp. 5-6) shares his agony on the existing pathetic scene of higher education system as a whole, thus:

> "Considering the abysmal degradation to which our educational institutions have fallen, one would wonder whether they could be redeemed at all. Perhaps the task is near impossible one. Yet, one cannot lose hope. There have been many instances in history of nations and institutions transforming themselves from an apparently hopeless situation into one of unbelievable success and glory. What we need today is Perestroika, complete restructuring in our system of higher education".

One should be happy that Pylee had at least left a note of optimism for reformation. But who will reform whom? Where

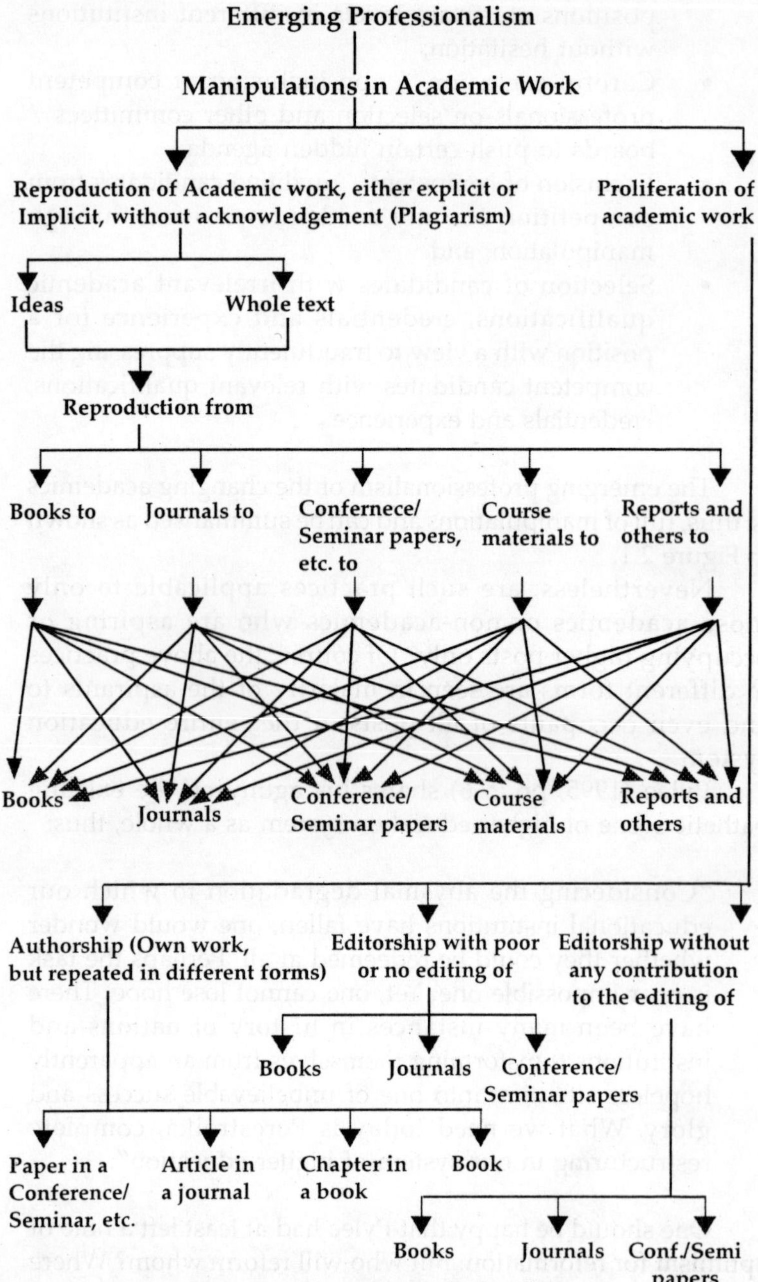

Figure 2.1 : Emerging Professionalism

to begin and end? No doubt, the task is difficult. Perhaps, this is the reason why Kapur (1999, pp. 10-11) has rather liberated the entire educational system in his article on "Our Liberated Educational System". His comments on 'liberated teachers' are interesting:

> "Every teacher is assured that on the day he joins a college or university he will be confirmed irrespective of his performance.... Thanks to the Merit Promotion Scheme of the UGC, he also feels that he will get promotions at regular intervals after some formalities of interviews, etc., are completed.... His standing in the profession will be determined by his seniority rather than by his teaching or by the results of his students. His mind is perfectly at ease and he can do whatever he likes, academic or un-academic and he is free to pursue his own interests."

In such a situation, who are desirable, the plagiarists or the 'liberated teachers'? Is there a third choice?

How to Reform?

Given the above state-of-the-art situation, where to start the reformation process? Goel and Goel (1999, pp. 10-11) suggest that:

> "Utmost care must be taken to select men of ability and experience to occupy the post of Vice-chancellor...... The Vice-chancellor, being the Chief Executive responsible for academic and administrative functions, in turn, must take utmost care to locate such people, who are rare birds, suitable for the respective functions".

Many have talked a lot about changes, reforms, etc. required for appointment of Vice-chancellors. But, we have to think about bringing in reforms that can help in arresting the professionalism of the plagiarists, amongst others, because the unchecked growth of unwanted literature in any discipline would lead to:

- Continuance and flourishing of plagiarists, the proliferation of practices of the 'emerging professionalism';
- Increasing assault on the brain of committed academics, who want to update themselves with the latest literature and developments, amongst doing other duties;
- Further fall of academic standards and discouragement to the genuinely committed academics and professionals;
- Quality deterioration in literature; and
- Maximum exploitation or misuse of the potential of information and communication technology by the plagiarists.

One can notice that the emerging professionalism of the changing academics is full of manipulations as depicted in Figure—2.1. This is also supported by relevant literature as we have seen. Are all these manipulations unfair, unacceptable and illegal? Obviously the answer is 'no'. But one should be able to distinguish between professionally fair and legally acceptable practices and those which are not. Certainly, steeling others' work / contributions or any one dishonestly appropriating others' intellectual property is not only condemnable and illegal but also punishable. Further, unnecessary proliferation or repetition of these practices in different ways and forms stands a strong testimony to professional and moral bankruptcy which would spell disaster to the whole process of intellectual enquiry and honesty.

It may be noted that the proliferation of one's own academic work, with a difference and with a view to elaborating it at different stages of its process falls in line with normal process of gradual addition of new knowledge and literature to the existing one in the relevant discipline and is not, therefore, an unacceptable practice. However, publication of ones own work ditto, without any change or reference to the previous work in different forms and at different times, is certainly an unnecessary addition, except that it provides access to wider audience. Yet, the academics concerned should restrain themselves from such manipulations and pave way for qualitative addition to knowledge with enhanced access, rather than quantitative addition which becomes a burden to existing knowledge and literature. But the major concern of the academic community should be to contain the emerging plagiarism, which passes for professionalism till it is exposed. It is well within the context here to look at the distinction between professionalism and professionalisation as referred to by Shah (1998). Professionalism is a long process by which an occupation succeeds over a period of time by meeting the criteria of a professional gamut. It includes improvement of status and professionality of knowledge and skills involved in one's practice (Peter, 1983, p. 205). According to Collins (1991, pp. 86-87) the term 'professionalism' describes a combination of serious commitment to the task at hand, competence, and a measure of self-directedness with a high concern for exclusive self interest. Professionalisation is a process of change in the direction of the ideal type; and as occupations professionalise, they undergo a sequence of structural changes involving the establishment of training institutions, professional organisations for mastery of theoretical knowledge, skills, etc.

In the light of the above distinction between professionalism and professionalisation, we have to see how plagiarism has assumed the character of professionalism and the plagiarists, to promote their self-interests, have transformed themselves as 'professionals' or 'academics'. At the same time, they have been increasingly collaborating with publishers, distributors and others who have money-making as their primary motive. Added to this, the people occupying high academic positions are giving their support by writing forewords, etc., to plagiarised works. It is high time that the professional plagiarists are recognised for what they are, so that genuine knowledge is not contaminated any further.

There should be very effective policies to punish the plagiarists and discourage their practices on one hand, and to improve academic standards on the other. There is, therefore, a need to evolve a code of punishment by the universities/ institutions concerned or by the appropriate authorities. The code should cover the plagiarists of all sorts such as teachers, academics, professionals, freelancers or others and those encouraging such practices, such as publishers or others. It should be comprehensive enough to punish the plagiarists for plagiarism, may be the ideas or text, of few sentences, a paragraph, a page, a chapter or entire document of any kind. In other words, it should cover all kinds of products of plagiarism wherein the books, journals, conference or seminar papers, course materials, reports and/or others must have served as sources.

The punishment can be minor which may be in the form of a warning or admonishment, or banning the plagiarised publication(s), imposition of fine or penalty, or a combination of these. The punishment can be major in terms of debarring the plagiarists from coming out with any such publications, suspension of the plagiarist(s) from the service wherever applicable followed by an enquiry, demotion in service, dismissal from service, or any other appropriate punishment depending upon the nature and extent of plagiarism. In other words, the magnitude of punishment should correspond to the nature and extent of plagiarism. Also, the time bound, fool-proof procedures are to be laid down for imposing minor and major punishments at national and international level, especially in the light of recent laws on intellectual property rights. Gupta (2001) and University News (1994) cite a number of cases of plagiarism in the disciplines of cardiology, chemistry, biochemistry, microbiology, mathematics, statistics, management, etc. resorted to by Professors, Heads of Departments, Scientists and others. The range of punishments inflicted on these plagiarists include: withdrawal of papers, tendering of unconditional apology, stripping of headships, demotion, suspension, termination from service and the like. While plagiarism is common in many parts of the world the punishment for the plagiarists has been serve only in advanced countries. In developing countries like India the professionalism of many plagiarists is either not noticed, or even if noticed it is not taken up seriously, or even if challenged seriously it has often gone unpunished. Irony is that there are even instances where the plagiarists have been promoted by the academic mafia and the cynical heads of institutions.

The proliferation of plagiarism in different forms and kinds is not a problem of one particular country. It has its implications for educational policies and practices, particularly recruitment, selection, placement or promotion of persons to different positions, beyond the country(ies) of origin. So, there must be stringent policies to arrest professionalism of plagiarists at different levels—institutional, national and international. But the primary and effective steps should start at the institutions concerned or in the domicile countries of the plagiarists. At the same time, a lot of responsibilities lie with the international community in exposing the plagiarists and their products so that there will be increased fear of punishment among the plagiarists and those promoting them on one hand, and greater demand or pressure on the appropriate authorities for imposition of punishment on the concerned on the other. Then only, one can expect some change in the changed (to the worse) and still changing academics and their practices.

Notes

1. A poster presented at Pan-Commonwealth Forum on Open Learning held at Brunei Darussalam from 1-5 March, 1999, the discussion on it, and suggestions for incorporation of evidences in the form of references, amongst others, have formed the basis for this chapter.
2. For more details of evidence regarding different kinds of plagiarism and punishments, see Lakshmi Reddy (1998), Ambirajan (1998), University News (1994) and Gupta (2001) given under the references to follow.

References

Ambirajan, S. (1998). View from the Periphery: Plagiarising Professors. *The Economic Times* (A daily newspaper published in English). New Delhi: The Economic Times, November 10, 1998.

Asha, S. Kanwar (1995). Distance Education for Women's Empowerment, in Asha, S. Kanwar and Neela, J. (eds) *Speaking for Ourselves: Women and Distance Education in India,* New Delhi: Manohar Publishers and Distributors.

Bakhshish Singh. (1994). Mechanism of Maintenance of Standards in Distance Education. In Murali Manohar, (ed) (pp. 1-7), *Distance Education in India: Studies in Quality and Quantitative Aspects.* Warangal: Indian Distance Education Association.

—. (1995). Mechanisms of Maintenance of Standards in Distance Education. In Bakhshish Singh, (ed) (pp. 189-194), *New Horizons in Distance Education,* New Delhi: Uppal Publishing House.

Brahmaji Rao, S. (1993). Staff Development through Distance Education: An Alternative Mode. A paper presented at *First National Conference of Indian Distance Education Association on Quality of Distance Education* held at Warangal: Organised by School of Distance Learning and Continuing Education, Kakatiya University, From 3-5 November, 1993.

—.(1994a). Staff Development through Distance Education: An Alternative Mode. In K. Murali Manohar, (ed), (pp. 117-124). *Staff Training in Distance Education.* Warangal: School of Distance Learning and Continuing Education, Kakatiya University.

—.(1994b). Staff Development through Distance Education: An Alternative Mode. In Dr. BRAOU, (ed), (pp. 66-76). *Distance Education: An Interface.* Hyderabad: Dr. BRAOU.

Collins, M. (1991). Adult Education as Vocation. London: Routledge. Quoted in S.Y. Shah. (1998). Professionalisation of Indian Adult Education. *University News,* 36(42), 6-10.

DDE (Division of Distance Education) (1989): *Readings in Distance Education - I* (A Collection of Papers Presented at Various Occasions by Prof. Ram Reddy), New Delhi: Indira Gandhi National Open University (IGNOU).

DDE (1994). Growth and Present Status, Block I of DE - I, *Growth and Philosophy of Distance Education,* New Delhi: IGNOU, December.

Gao, F. (1991). The Challenge of Distance Education in China, *The American Journal of Distance Education,* 5(2).

Gentai, G., Farnes, N., and Woodley, A. (1993). Network Models for Distance Education in Hungary, *Open Learning,* 8(2), June.

Goel, A & Goel, S.L. (1999). Vice-chancellor's Appointment: Need for Successor Planning, *University News,* 37(44), 10-12.

Gupta, Y.P. (2001). Plagiarising Research Data. *The Hindu* (An English daily newspaper), New Delhi: The Hindu, January 23.

Kamala, B.K. (1994). Women-friendly Perspectives on Distance Education: Problems and Prospects with Special reference to Indian conditions. In Dr. BRAOU, (ed) (pp. 26-33), *op cit.*

—.(1995). Women-friendly Perspectives on Distance Education: Problems and Prospects in India. In Bakhshish Singh (ed), (pp. 134-140), *op cit.*

Kapur, J.N. (1999). Our Liberated Educational System. *University News,* 37(50), 10-12.

Khurana, R., Kaushik, M., and Yadava, K. (1993). *Marketing of Services: Concepts and Applications,* New Delhi: School of Management Studies, IGNOU.

Lakshmi Reddy, M.V. (1996a). A Scientific Approach to Organising Counselling for Distance Learners. A paper presented at *IV Annual Conference of Indian Distance Education Association on Learner to the Learner: Developing improved Strategies toward Better Student Support Services,* held at Hyderabad: November 22-24, 1996.

—.(1996b). A Scientific Approach to Organising Counselling for Distance Learners. *Kakatiya Journal of Open Learning*, 2(2), 66-81.

—.(1998). A Book Review—Manjulika S., and Venugopal Reddy, V. (1996). Distance Education in India: A Model for Developing Countries, New Delhi: Vikas Publishing House Pvt. Ltd., Pp. 255 + xviii, price Rs. 350/- (Hard bound). *Journal of Educational Planning and Administration*, 12(2), 229-232.

—.(1999). Changing Academics and Emerging Professionalism in Distance Education. A poster presented at the *Pan-Commonwealth Forum on Open Learning: Empowerment through Knowledge and Technology*held at Brunei Darussalam: Organised by Commonwealth of Learning, Canada from 1-5 March, 1999.

Mohan Rao, C.K. & Lakshmi Reddy, M.V. (1992). Feedback Study on Daily Newspapers, Broadsheet for Neo-literates. A paper presented at a *Seminar on Role of Libraries in Adult Education*held at New Delhi: Organised by Indian Adult Education Association in collaboration with National Book Trust on February 8, 1992.

—.(1996). Feedback Study on Daily Newspapers, Broadsheet for Neo-literates. In Venkatappaiah, V. (ed) (pp. 170-174), *Literacy Campaign and Libraries*. New Delhi: ESS ESS Publications.

Panda, S.K. (ed) (1997a, 1998a, 1999a), *Staff and Educational Development International*, 1(1-3), 2(1-3), & 3(1-2).

—. (1997b, 1998b, 1999b, 2000), *Indian Journal of Open Learning*. (6(1-3), 7(1-3), 8(1-3), & 9(1).

Peter Jarvis. (1983). *Adult Continuing Education: Theory and Practice*. London: Croom Helm. Quoted in S.Y. Shah, op cit.

Prasad, V.S. (1992). Dr. B.R. Ambedkar Open University: A Decennial Perspective, *Indian Journal of Open Learning*, 1(2), July.

Prasad, V.S. (1994). Staff Training and Development in Distance Education: Dr. BRAOU Experience. In Dr. BRAOU, (ed), (pp. 60-65), *op cit*.

—. (1995). Staff Training and Development in Distance Education: Dr. BRAOU Experience. In Bakhshish Singh, (ed), (pp. 202-208), *op cit*.

Pylee, M.V. (1995). Reforming Higher Education. *University News*. October 16, 1995. Quoted in A. Goel and S.L. Goel, *op cit*.

Raja Mouli, C. (1994) Networking of Distance Learning Institutions in India: Promises for the Future. In Dr. BRAOU, (ed) (pp. 49-53), *op cit*.

—. (1995). Networking of Distance Learning Institutions in India: Promises for the Future. In Bakshish Singh, (ed) (pp. 254-258), *op cit*.

Ramanujam, P.R. (1995). *Reflections on Distance Education for India*. New Delhi: Manak Publications (P) Ltd.

RSD (Regional Services Division) (1989). *Manual for Coordinators of Study Centres*, New Delhi: IGNOU.

RSD (1992). *Manual for Regional Directors*, New Delhi: IGNOU.
Rumble, G. (1989). 'Open Learning', 'Distance Learning', and the Misuse of Language, *Open Learning*, 4(2), June.
Sarup, A. (1999). Management of Universities: Retrospect and Prospect. *University News*. 37(9). Quoted in A. Goel and S.L. Goel, op cit.
Shah, S.Y. (1998). Professionalisation of Indian Adult Education. *University News*, 36(42), 6-10.
Singh, R.K. (1996). Revamping Higher Education System. *University News*. February 12, 1996. Quoted in A. Goel and S.L. Goel op cit.
SOE (School of Education) (1992). Modern Media for Distance Education, Block-2 of ES-318, *Communication Technology for Distance Education*, New Delhi: IGNOU, February.
Subba Rao, U. (1994). Management of Student Support Services in Open University. In Dr. BRAOU, (ed), (pp. 100-105), *op cit*.
—. (1995). Management of Student Support Services in Open University. In Bakhshish Singh, (ed), (pp. 86-90), *op cit*.
Takwale, Ram, G. (1994). Application of New Technologies in Distance Education. In Dr. BRAOU, (ed), (pp. i-xii), *op cit*.
—. (1995). Application of New Technologies in Distance Education. In Bakhshish Singh, (ed), (pp. 45-56), *op cit*.
University News (1994). Vol. XXXII, No.17, April 25.
Walter, R. Sharp. (1961). Field Administration in the UN system. London: Routledge. Quoted in A. Goel and S.L. Goel *op cit*.

3

Teachers and Academics in Distance and Open Learning Institutions

Teaching through distance mode is different from classroom teaching. The collective nature of distance teaching demands from academics varied functions. Both academic and administrative functions at an Open University get mixed up, and the concept of pure teaching has little relevance here. However, the tasks related to course development and its delivery can be carried out with sensitivity by academics only. Course or programme development and delivery in distance education is a well co-ordinated team work involving teachers and other academics at different levels. These teachers and other academics are employed on full-time, part-time, permanent and/or temporary basis and have wide ranging designations that vary from an institute to an institute in a country or across the countries. It is, perhaps, needless to make general list of designations of these teachers and academics because it does not serve any purpose here. But, by looking at the contributions made by them to many course materials of various open and distance education institutions, one can notice that they perform common functions and that there is very little difference between the quantity and quality of their contributions to course development and delivery. This may be almost common with any open and distance learning institution in most of the developing countries at least.

A word on the magnitude of these teachers and academics in India. There are about 40,000 teachers and academics, part-time and full-time, in 10 Open Universities (DEC, 2000). In addition, there can be around 5000 teachers/academics associated or employed full-time and/part-time with 62 Directorates/Institutes of Distance Education (DDEs/IDEs) located in dual mode institutions.

It is a well known fact that the teachers and academics working with dual mode Universities have been getting stepmotherly treatment from their counterparts involved in face-to-face teaching of conventional programmes in the same University. And the Correspondence Course Institutions or Directorates of Distance Education have been suffering for want of financial, academic and administrative autonomy amongst others (Bakhshish Singh, et al., 1994).

Nevertheless, the situation of teachers and academics in majority of distance and open learning institutions in India is almost alike, except for certain better facilities and privileges available to them in certain institutions. But, it is interesting to find differential treatment meted out to academic staff, in the name of 'teachers', 'academics', 'other academics' and so on even in the single mode universities such as Open Universities. In view of their common situation this Chapter basically attempts to present the retrospect and prospect of teachers and other academics in one representative institution i.e., the Indira Gandhi National Open University (IGNOU) in India.

Teachers and other academics at IGNOU are engaged in a variety of activities, but they are basically academics engaged in teaching, research and related activities. The functional difference between a 'teacher' and 'other academic' is quite often mistaken. This Chapter also seeks to clarify some of the issues related to teachers and other academics at IGNOU.

Indira Gandhi National Open University (IGNOU) formally came into existence in September, 1985 by an Act of Parliament (No. 50 of 1985). Within a decade of its existence the university has established itself and assumed the size of a national 'giant' in the Indian system of higher education by stretching its limits to the length and breadth of the nation. It has rather heralded a new era in the University education. The University has set up 9 schools, 10 divisions, 2 Centres, a Staff Training and Research Institute in Distance Education (STRIDE), and Distance Education Council (DEC) at its Headquarters in New Delhi. Besides these, IGNOU has 26 Regional Centres and 504 Study Centres in different States and Union Territories. Having made the beginning of its academic life in 1987, the University has launched 39 programmes and developed 486 courses till date (IGNOU, 2000). These programmes lead to certificate, diploma or degree (graduate or post-graduate or research) in various disciplines. Many programmes are offered in the medium of English and Hindi. Some programmes are being offered in many Indian languages as well. The above achievements, among many others, raised the reputation of the University at national and international level. Within 8 years of its existence it rose to the level of getting the distinction of the *Centre of Excellence in Distance Education* conferred on it in 1993 by the Commonwealth of Learning, Canada. It is also one of the ten mega Open Universities in the World (IGNOU, 1996).

Sine the inception, the University has been making untiring efforts to diversify and strengthen higher education in India through distance education mode. In the pursuit of this gigantic task it becomes inevitable for it to face many challenges and problems—internal and external, in and outside its system. The internal and external problems mostly relate to the university in general, the employees and students in particular. The external challenges come up during its dealings with other educational and non-educational institutions in and outside India. These problems and challenges may be sudden, foreseen and unforeseen, perceived or unperceived. The University can be successful in facing the external challenges and the internal problems, particularly those strongly felt by both employees and the employer, if they are tackled effectively and logically through appropriate mechanisms.

The matters, issues and problems related to the employees, and of academics in particular of any educational institution have important implications for its smooth functioning, academic output and efficiency. IGNOU is no exception to it. An attempt is made here to analyse and highlight the major internal problems and issues faced by teachers and academics of the University which are sequel to its decisions regarding their status and prospects. These problems and issues, if not addressed timely and properly, would have greater bearing on the job satisfaction of its teachers and academics, on tapping their competencies, capabilities, etc., and thus on their academic contribution to the University and the nation at large.

Teachers and Other Academics in IGNOU

One of the major issues related to the staffing pattern at IGNOU is the distinction between the terms 'teachers' and 'other academics'. Before discussing the situation of 'teachers' and 'other academics' and their prospects at IGNOU it would be appropriate to look at what a *'teacher'* and an 'academic' in general, is. A *'teacher'* is a person or a thing that teaches or instructs; one whose occupation and ability is to instruct or to impart knowledge, practical skills, and understanding (Murrey et. al.,1978; Webster, 1986; Kirkpatrick, 1986; Brown, 1993). Barrow and Milburn (1986; 221), however, observe that "teaching is a broad, general term. It is sometimes referred to as a polymorphus (many-sided) word, since it may encompass a wide variety of more specific activities such as lecturing, instructing, drilling, eliciting responses, asking questions, testing, providing information, encouraging and conducting seminars".

An *'academic'* is a member of the teaching/research staff of an educational institution i.e., the academic staff as opposed to the support staff. In the United States, *'faculty'* refers to members of the academic staff who are employed by the university or other educational institution (Jarvis, 1990). An academic is "one studying or teaching at a University especially one who has scholarly tastes" (Kirkpatrick, 1986). An academic is "a member of the University or similar institution or a person engaged or excelling in scholarly pursuits" (Brown, 1993).

From the above definitions of 'teacher' and 'academic' it can be understood that the work of a teacher includes, a wide variety of things and activities. The word 'academic' thus includes a teacher and/or researcher of an educational institution engaged or excelling in scholarly pursuits. It is, thus, very obvious that teachers are rather a part or one specific group of academic staff of an educational organisation.

In the light of the above definitions of 'teacher' and 'academic', the author would like to explain the concept of 'teachers' and 'academics' at IGNOU. The term "teachers" is more comprehensively defined in the IGNOU Act, 1985 (Section 2(P)) and falls almost in line with that of Barrow and Milburn. It permits inclusion of all categories of persons participating in the process of guiding and assisting students within the meaning of the expression 'teachers'.

The distance education system requires the services of certain specialist personnel who may not be teachers or administrators in the traditional sense. They would be performing a wide spectrum of functions which combine managerial or administrative competence with academic sensitivity and understanding. The performance of such intermediate level functions and development of a category of specialist personnel for the purpose is necessary for the success of the distance education system (Takwale, 1991:3). IGNOU, of course, is a University with a difference and hence its teachers and academics also should be different. Obviously, when such type of staff are to be recruited and selected for the system it is necessary that a well thought out staffing procedure is formulated before starting the process of selection of personnel for these positions. Moreover, the selection committee should have the experts with suitable qualifications and relevant experience to select candidates to such positions. But , in practice, it is often otherwise for various reasons.

These academics at IGNOU can broadly be classified under three categories viz., (i) Academics in Schools; (ii)

Academics in Divisions; and (iii) Academics in Regional Services. The Schools of Studies and Divisions are located at the Headquarters at New Delhi while the Regional Centres are located in different parts of the country, mostly in the capital cities of the States and Union Territories. In fact, academics in Schools are called 'teachers' with different designations—Professors, Readers and Lecturers. Of course, the category of Academic Associates who were previously employed in the Schools have been abolished by the University for various reasons. Moreover, the paramount services rendered by these Academic Associates in the early years of the University have not been properly counted in promoting their career and interests at later stages. However, research staff with different designations do exist in some Schools and Divisions. The University has academics posted in some of the Divisions at the Headquarters. The Regional Services Division is an important Division which co-ordinates the activities of Regional Centres. Further, its part-time academics—the Co-ordinators, Assistant Co-ordinators and Academic Counsellors—belong to the conventional Universities in different States and Union Territories and are available at the Study Centre, Programme Centre or Work Centre only. According to IGNOU profile (2000) the strength of its academics in its broadest sense is 294 full-time teachers/academics and 20,000 part-time academic counsellors.

Notwithstanding the above, the University had, till recently, a unique category called the *"Other Academics"*. This is a category which does not exist in this form in any other educational/research institutions in India or abroad and this will be dealt with later at some length.

The wide-spread opinion among the non-teaching or non-academic staff of the University is that all the academics in IGNOU discharge only quasi-academic duties. In other words, the non-academic staff feel that they too do these duties at times. This opinion has, perhaps, some force in view of the nature, stage and status of the University. An admitted fact is that most of the academics in the Schools, Divisions and Regional Centres are, most often, expected to do some work of non-academic nature. Keeping in view the nature, stage and status of the University as stated above and its needs, the kind of problems the teachers and academics are now facing need to be addressed after a thorough consideration of various relevant documents such as the IGNOU Act, Statutes, Ordinances, Rules, Office Orders, etc., vis-à-vis their present status. Teachers and academics come into the organisation through a proper selection procedure specifically laid down for the purpose. Besides this, the nature of duties a particular category of employees discharge matters much in calling that particular category of employees as teachers or academics.

Academic Activities at IGNOU

The academic activities / functions at IGNOU can broadly be classified into three types (Takwale, 1991):

(a) Development of discipline-based courses and programmes;
(b) Delivery of programmes / various services to students; and
(c) Research and development of systems and procedures.

All the above types of activities are equally important in an Open University. One without the other is ineffective. The *first* type of functions / activities are carried out by the Schools of Studies. The functions of this type include: preparation of course / programmes, maintenance of courses and bringing out revised versions or editions of courses. But the academic processes in distance education do not end with preparation of learning packages. Regional Services Division in co-operation and co-ordination with other Divisions and Schools concerned carry out the *second* type of functions which include: identification, mobilisation and involvement of local resources to deliver the programmes, provision for guidance and counselling services to students, monitoring and evaluation of their assignments, awarding certificates, diplomas, degrees, etc. The *third* type of functions are carried out by different Divisions and Schools, either independently in the areas of their functions or jointly by Schools and/or Divisions as is required for the betterment of the system and procedures. These functions include the rest of the academic functions like preparation and production of audio / video programmes, evaluation of students' performance, systems development, programme evaluation, planning, editing of the material, translation, library and documentation, etc. To be brief, the first two types of functions above are discharged solely by the academics at Schools of Studies, Regional Services Division and Regional Centres of the University. The third type of activities form a part of the responsibilities of all the Schools and Divisions of the University.

For a better understanding of the prospect and retrospect of teachers and other academics in the University, it is important to look at the statutory provisions in the IGNOU Act pertaining to them and the manner in which these provisions were implemented, interpreted and enforced. This would also help in understanding better the magnitude of wastage or inappropriate use of its academic resources.

The IGNOU Act and Statutes

The gist of some of the provisions of the IGNOU Act, hereinafter called the Act, and the ambiguities in interpreting them are presented below for a thorough understanding of the situation in which teachers and other academics are placed.

As per the IGNOU Act, the terms can be described as:

(i) "Teachers" means Professors, Readers, and Lecturers and such other persons as may be designated as such by the University. (Section 2(P) of the Act).

(ii) The University shall have the power to institute some academic positions other than Professors, Readers

and Lecturers and appoint persons to the same positions. (Section 5(1) (vi) of the Act.

(iii) The constitution of the Selection Committee is same for all academic positions, which includes teaching and such other academic positions. (Statute 12 (2) (i) of the Act).

(iv) Appointment of academics is by means of a written contract with the persons selected. (Statute 17 (2) of the Act.

(v) Service conditions of all academics are similar, unless the contract is otherwise entered into with any individual or group of academics. (Statute 17 (1) of the Act).

(vi) There are two categories of employees *(a)* Teachers and other academics, *(b)* employees other than teachers and other academics, i.e., *(a)* academic category—includes teachers as well and *(b)* non-academic category (Statute 18 of the Act).

These sections and provisions of the Act and statutes are given completely in the notes at the end of this Chapter. It can be clearly observed from these provisions of the Act and Statutes that:

(i) The words "teachers and other academics" come together at many places in the Act and these words should be read together instead of breaking them into "teachers" and "other academics".

(ii) The term 'academics' includes the teachers and other groups of academics. The teacher groups of academics have been defined clearly in the Act and there are many more academic positions that have to be identified and instituted. It means that the "teachers and other academics" are one and the same category i.e., "academics".

(iii) All the provisions are very consistent and they mean that there are not two categories such as "teachers" and "other academics", but it is only one category with different groups of academics, of which

"teachers" as defined in the Act form or belong to one group of academics.

(iv) If the University completes its task of identifying, designating and instituting all the academic positions other than the specified "teacher" group of academics the very question of "other academics" as a separate category does not arise and these very words become redundant. In other words, as soon as any academic position other than the positions of teachers' (identified and clearly defined as Professors, Readers and Lecturers in the Act) is created and the person is appointed, that position cannot be called "other academic" as it has already become academic with a specific designation assigned to it, which could not be contemplated, identified and defined exhaustively in the Act.

Enforcement of the Act and Statutes

In the light of the factual position of the aforesaid provisions of the Act and Statutes, it is very interesting to look at how these provisions have been enforced. This also reflects the way in which the academics in the country have been attracted and how their faculties and resources have been under-used.

In pursuance of Sections 2 and 5 of the Act, the University identified, designated and instituted some academic positions other than teachers positions. These include : Director (D), Joint Director(JD), Deputy Director(DD), Assistant Director(AD) in the Regional Services Division amongst other Divisions and Centres at the Headquarters, and Regional Director(RD), and Assistant Regional Director(ARD) in the Regional Centres. The University followed the University Grants Commission's guidelines in fixing the qualifications for various academic positions at par with those requisite for the posts of Lecturers, Readers and Professors and accordingly appointed persons to these positions. Subsequently, the University appointed committees like Rais Ahmed Committee, Takwale Committee, etc. and came out with unique title, the "Other Academic Staff" in 1992 for all these positions in Regional Services Division and Regional Centres amongst others. Thus, academics in IGNOU have been dissected into two categories—'Teachers' and 'Other Academics'. Nonetheless, it is surprising to note that the appointing authority of all these "Other Academic Staff" in Regional Services and the "teachers" in the Schools is the Director, Teacher Affairs Division, recently renamed as Academic Co-ordination Division. The self-appraisal form used to assess the performance of all these academics at the time of confirmation is also one and the same.

However, one category of teachers (Lecturers), interviewed to test the discipline-based knowledge and selected accordingly by one and the same Selection Committee for the post of Lecturer, are posted with different designations—Lecturers (in Schools), Assistant Directors (in Regional Services Division) and Assistant Regional Directors (in Regional Centres). There are no stated criteria for posting of a person in the School/RC/RSD from the common panel of candidates so selected for the post of Lecturer. This discretion in posting of a selected candidate caused all the discrimination in their status (teacher or other academics), duties, terms and conditions of service, privileges, advantages and disadvantages attached to these designations though these positions are interchangeable. For instance, a Lecturer in a School is entitled for a vacation of two months a year while Assistant Directors and Assistant Regional Directors are not entitled to the same. If any Lecturer in a School is transferred, either suo-motto by the University or after obtaining the consent or at the request of the employee, to a Regional Centre or to Regional Services Division even by retaining his/her Lecturer designation (s)he forgoes certain benefits, privileges, facilities, particularly vacation attached to the position of 'Lecturer'. Contrary to this, a Lecturer, ARD, or AD in Regional Services if transferred to a School (s)he gets all the benefits at par with a Lecturer in a School. It is very difficult to understand the logic behind it.

When the employee is in an intertransferable position, can his conditions of services be subject to change with transfer? Can a Lecturer in a School and his counterpart at the Regional Services Division, or at the Regional Centres have different conditions of service though they have come from the same panel selected by the same selection committee for one and the same post? Can the selection of a teacher and any other academic be done by one and the same Selection Committee, if these are two different categories? This was further confounded by adding to this 'other academic' category a few more categories of employees selected by different selection committees. These include the positions of Analysts, Research Officers, Producers, Senior Producers and so on. Even if it is so, can the service conditions of the other groups of academics specified above be defined or modified subsequent to their appointment? Added to this, now, even among the ARDs there are two different cadres each selected through a different selection procedure, but discharging similar duties subject to the same conditions of service. The University had been making tireless attempt to clear the confusion but with little success. In fact, the attempts led to more of confusion than clarity.

A word on vacation to the academics in IGNOU. The teacher in a distance education performs a role altogether different from that of his conventional counterpart. Neither he has the students on regular basis for face-to-face interaction nor does he deliver any lecture in the classroom. All his teaching is, basically, through developing proper course material-in print, audio and/or video. However, the job of a teacher, be a Lecturer, Reader or Professor in distance education system, does not end with development or production of course material. It is, perhaps, half of the distance teacher's job. Here comes the role of academics other than the teachers to perform the other half of the distance teacher's job i.e., the delivery to the distance learner of the course material developed by one group of teachers performing only half of the distance teacher's job. Teaching in distance education is complete only when the course content, in whatever form it is produced, is delivered to the satisfaction of the learner. The point here is that the hitherto so called 'teachers'—Lecturers, Readers and Professors—are "not the complete teachers" in the sense that they do only half the job of distance teacher and the rest of the half is performed by the academics, other than teachers, available at different levels—Headquarters, and Regional and Study Centres. Therefore, in view of the nature of (distance) education the University offers, the absence of students on regular basis on its campus and the non-vacational nature of the University, is the extension of the facility of vacation to the so called "teachers" of IGNOU justified on any ground? If yes, on the same ground(s), are the academics other than the so called "teachers" not entitled for the same? Is it not essential to maintain the parity of this service condition for the "other half of the distance teachers" who form the complimentary academic category of the distance or open education system? Though the words "teachers and other academics" have been divided and interpreted as two categories, namely, "teachers" and "other academics" now the "other academic" category is called, through University's Board's decision as "academic". Thus, there are now "teachers" and "academic" categories. One basic question that still persists is: are teachers not a part of academics? If yes, why is this dichotomy of "teachers" and "academics" even today? All these have formed, often, a matter of daily discussions and controversy among the present, so called teachers and academics.

Now, to the intertransferability of academics. It is at present confined to Lecturer level category only. If the "teachers and other academics" are treated as one broad category i.e., the "academics" and the intertransferability is made applicable to the positions of Readers, Deputy Directors and Regional Directors, the three equivalent positions in the Schools, Regional Services Division and Regional Centres respectively, it would not only promote equality among its academics of this category as well but also promote healthy practice. Further, the Professor grade positions in the Regional Centres and the Regional Services Division and the positions of Professors in the Schools of Studies should be made intertransferable in order to maintain parity among the academics and the national character of the University. However, there is every need to maintain uniformity in selection procedure, their terms and conditions of service, including vacation in respect of all the intertransferable academic positions. The transfers between the academics in Schools, Regional Services Division at Headquarters and the Regional Centres should be periodical and compulsory. It would undoubtedly curtail the excessive involvement of academics, more particularly those at Headquarters, in extra-academic activities such as those of Teachers' Association and other petty matters hampering academic atmosphere and output. All the more, it would not only reflect its national character but also promote right attitude and work culture among the academics in the University.

Conclusion

To conclude, the kind of efforts put by the University to attract highly qualified and competent academics from all over the country are, no doubt, laudable. These academics are potent enough to bring more laurels such as "Centre of Excellence in Distance Education" to it. But the manner in which their academic competence is being rendered obsolete by inadequate and improper utilisation of the same is undoubtedly a tremendous waste of the human resources. Not only that the academics selected after thorough national level screening are not utilised properly by the Schools of Studies of the University in developing the courses in relevant disciplines, but also there is a lot of financial wastage in terms of travel and other allowances, remuneration etc., being paid for the academics invited for the purpose from other Colleges and Universities. Moreover, some of these invited academics who submit poor quality course material doubly tax the concerned teachers in respective Schools. The compelling reasons of the Schools to ignore its own qualified and competent academics and search for the same outside the University, may be as Senior or Junior Consultants or in some other form, are, however, not totally unknown to many academics of the University. The more vivid among the prominent reasons are to effectively deprive the competent internal academics of the opportunity to contribute to the University on one hand and to promote sychophancy, to protect the incompetent and to favour some externals for various extraneous reasons on the other. Would it not be prudent for the University to tap the talent, expertise and resource of competent academics available in it before looking for the same outside it? Wastage of both the kind of resources, human (academic) and financial, is thus, highly undesirable for a country like India which requires the maximum utilisation of the resources to meet the educational needs of thousands of distant learners. Moreover, for the University, this kind of wastage—underutilisation, misutilisation and malutilisation of human resources—is not justified. And also the nation canot afford it. It is high time that the University acted judiciously to tap its academics' abilities and resources by according proper academic status and by paving ways for equal opportunity for all the academics to contribute their maximum to the University.

References

Bakhshish Singh, Saroj Mallick and Neelam Chaudhary. (1994). "Correspondence/Distance Education in India : Excerpts from A Research Report", *Indian Journal of Open Learning*, Vol.3, No.2, pp.1-25.

Barrow. R., and Milburn G. (1986). A Critical Dictionary of Educational Concepts : *An Appraisal of Selected Ideas and Issues in Educational Theory and Practice.*, Sussex: Wheatsheaf Books Ltd., Harvest Press. Publishing Group, p. 221.

Brown. L. (Ed): (1993). *The New Shorter Oxford English Dictionary on Historical Principals*. Oxford: Clarendon Press.

Distance Education Council (DEC). (2000). *Open Universities in India: Brief Information*, New Delhi: IGNOU.

Indira Gandhi National Open University Act 1985 (Act No.50 of 1985) and the Statutes of the University, New Delhi: IGNOU.

Indira Gandhi National Open University (IGNOU). (1996). *Vice-Chancellor's Report, Seventh Convocation*, 11 May, New Delhi: IGNOU.

IGNOU (2000) *IGNOU Profile,* New Delhi: IGNOU.

Jarvis. P. (1990). *An International Dictionary of Adult and Continuing Education,* London: Routledge.

Kirkpatrick, E.M. (Ed). (1986). *Chambers Twentieth Century Dictionary,* New Edition, New Delhi: Allied Publishers Private Ltd.

Murray, J.A.H., H Bradley, W.A. Craigie and C.T. Onions (Eds). (1978). *The Oxford English Dictionary,* Vol. XI, Oxford: Oxford University Press.

Takwale, B.G., (Chairman). (1991). *Report of the Committee on the Structure for the Academic and Student Support Services System of the University and the Pattern of its Staffing,* New Delhi: Planning and Development Division, IGNOU.

Webster, M. (1986) *Websters Third New International Dictionary of the English Language: Unabridged with Seven Language Dictionary* Chicago: Encyclopedia Britannica, Inc.

Notes

1. Section 2 (p). "Teachers" means Professors, Readers, Lecturers, and such other persons as may be designated as such by way of the Ordinances for imparting instruction in the University or for giving guidance or rendering assistance to students for pursuing any course of study of the University.
2. Section 5 (1) (vi). The University shall have powers to institute Professorships, Readerships, Lectureships and other academic positions necessary for imparting instruction or for preparing educational material or for conducting other academic activities, including guidance, designing and delivery of course and evaluation of the work done by the students, and to appoint persons to such professorships, readerships, lectureships and other academic positions.
3. Statute 12 (2) (i). Each of the Selection committees for appointment to the post of Professors, Readers, Lecturers and the academic staff shall consist of the following members namely: *(a)* The Vice-chancellor; *(b)* a Pro-vice-chancellor or the Director of the School concerned nominated by the Vice-chancellor; *(c)* a person nominated by the visitor; and *(d)* three experts not in the service of the University to be nominated by the Vice-chancellor in such manner as may be specified in the ordinances.
4. Statute 17 (1). All the teachers and other academic staff of the university shall, in the absence of any contract to the contrary, be governed by the terms and conditions of service and code of conduct as are specified in the statutes and the ordinances.
5. Statute 17 (2). Every teacher and member of other academic staff of the university shall be appointed on a written contract, the form of which shall be specified in the statutes.
6. Statute 18. All the employees of the University, other than the teachers and other academic staff of the university, shall, in the absence of any contract to the contrary, be governed by the terms and conditions of service and code of conduct as are specified in the statutes and ordinances.

7. Indira Gandhi National Open University's Circular F. No. 1-III/Admn-Gen/Teachers/88/2778 dated 2 June, 1992 classified the Group 'A' positions—Director, Joint Director, Deputy Director, Asstt. Director in Regional Services Division and Regional Director and Assistant Regional Director in Regional Centres of the University—as 'Other Academic Staff' and specified qualifications required by the candidates for appointment to these positions.

Section - II

Bettering the Delivery of Programmes

4

Dropouts: An Overview

Distance and open education institutions take pride in the number of students registered every year or the total number of students on rolls. For example, the number of students registered for the academic year 2000 in 10 open universities in India is 472,102 while total number of students on rolls as on January 2000 of these Universities is 1,353,054. But these institutions have paid little attention to the problem of dropouts and failures. In other words, the percentage of pass-outs to the total on rolls has been very insignificant. For instance, the number of pass-outs in the year 1999 was 52,255. This means the percentage of pass-outs to the total number of students on rolls in the year 1999 is about 6% only. From this one can understand the magnitude and intensity of the problem of not only dropouts, but also non-starters and failures which is 94% to the total number of students on rolls in the relevant year. In this chapter an attempt is made to provide an overview of the problem of dropouts in distance and open learning institutions. Of course, the studies covered in this chapter are not exhaustive and there may be studies which the author could not have access to or has not come across. The overview presents global picture with focus on dropouts in India.

It is undisputed fact that the distance learners differ from one another in their socio-economic background, age, educational qualifications, experience and so on. They may or may not have an understanding of distance education prior to their enrolment or registration in any distance education programme. Whatever be the case, some initial motivation and enthusiasm must have persuaded them to enroll or register for the distance education programme or course. This initial motivation and enthusiasm of the distance learners should not be shattered by problems, difficulties and unmet needs in pursuing the programme or course, because these together might ultimately lead to their dropping out, poor performance or failures.

If the personal problems such as conflict between study and work, insufficient commitment etc. are the major hurdles for the distance learners in pursuing the programme/course or for their dropout, there is not much for the distance education institution to worry. Yet, it can attempt to find solutions to their personal problems even. But, if the problems connected with the distance education institution or the programme are the major ones for dropping out, poor performance, failure, etc. then there is a major concern for the institution. There is a need to identify the nature and character of the programme from which the dropout rate is more, the point or time of their dropout or withdrawal from the programme/course, the characteristics and nature of dropouts, the reasons for dropping out or withdrawal, and so on. These questions call for an overview of the dropout problem vis-à-vis the above aspects. This assumes greater significance in distance education as it would help in enabling the distance education institution to understand the problems of distance learners better and in developing suitable measures, policies or packages, to prevent or reduce dropouts.

Focus

There is a need to study the state-of-the-art research on dropout with a view to identifying the nature of the programme(s) from which the distance learners dropout, the point or time of withdrawal, dropout or attrition, the nature and characteristics of dropouts, and the reasons for their dropout. Of course, the problems, difficulties and unmet felt needs of learners of a particular programme of one distance education institution may differ from those of another institution in a particular country or institutions across the countries.

A look at the dropouts studies with this perspective would give better understanding of the problem and an insight into finding meaningful solutions to the problem of dropout. Hence, the chapter also attempts to present its global perspective on the above aspects and to come out with meaningful suggestion(s) on the problem. This is very important and useful to address the issues of high rates of dropout occurring in a particular year or in a particular course or programme.

It would be appropriate to begin with the definition of 'dropout'.

Definition of Dropout

It is important to define the term 'dropout' because it helps in understanding the problem clearly and in focusing on the concerns in the area effectively by setting proper parameters. Of course, the distance education literature abounds with terms such as wastage, failure, dropout and withdrawal. 'Attrition' is another term used in some American and Australian writings. Terms like rejected undergraduates, student mortality and retirement are also used occasionally (Roberts, 1984). The concept of dropout is not clearly defined in the context of distance education in India or even in other countries and therefore serious investigations into dropout in distance education are yet to be undertaken (Murali Manohar, 1994, p. 77). However, there is scanty research done on dropouts in Indian correspondence courses.

Peters (1992) defines dropout as a student who does not sit for examinations. Eisenberg and Dowsett (1990) define dropouts as finally registered students who have withdrawn from the course before the final examination. But according to Fan and Chan (1997) the dropouts are those who did decide not to continue and did not submit any work since then and did not take their examinations. They also distinguish these dropouts from initial dropouts. They define initial dropouts as those students who do not submit any work to the institution.

Roberts (1984) attempts to define dropout by classifying dropouts into the following three classes of students.

(i) The student who informs the institution that he/she no longer wishes to continue studying;

(ii) The student who is prevented from continuing studies by the institution because of failure to satisfy institutional regulations such as not meeting standards necessary for minimum rate of progression; and

(iii) The student who disappears and fails to respond to all forms of follow-up procedures initiated by the institution.

For the purpose of this chapter, the terms, 'dropout', 'withdrawal' and 'attrition' are treated as synonymous. With due regard to the context in which these terms have been defined, each of the definitions offered by Roberts (1984), Eisenberg and Dowsett (1990), Peters (1992) and Fan and Chan (1997) is considered as appropriate and adequate by itself.

In addition to these, I would like to give a general definition that encompasses all contexts of the problem. The dropout is a properly registered student who has either withdrawn himself from the course or programme of study at any point of time either by informing or not informing the institution of his intention to withdraw, or has been prevented by the institution for not satisfying the institutional regulations at any point during the course of the programme.

Time or Point of Dropout

The point or time at which there is high rate of dropout, withdrawal or attrition gives an understanding of the intensity of the problems of students in pursuing the programme. This would also give an idea of time or period for institutional intervention to bring down the rate of dropout, withdrawal, attrition or even failure and to improve performance of students. Therefore, it would be appropriate to look at the research evidence on the point or time of withdrawal, dropout or attrition.

Brandt (1956) found that more than half of the withdrawals occurring at the United States Armed Forces Institute of External Studies did not submit their first lesson and were dis-enrolled within six months of starting. James and Wedemeyer (1959) found that 93% of all dropouts from the University of Wisconsin had withdrawn before completing a quarter of the programme.

Harter (1969) reports that 34% of all students enrolled never submitted any work for credit and that 75% of all withdrawals had occurred before the students had completed a quarter of their studies at State University of New York.

Sheath (1965) reports that in the University of New England, Australia the withdrawal rate during the first year of a programme normally lasting six years was approximately 40% of the total withdrawal for the external course. Roberts (1980) studied dropout pattern at a small college of Advanced Education in New South Wales, Australia and showed that 93% of students who failed to graduate had withdrawn prior to enrolling in the second semester of a four semester programme. Roberts (1984) points out that the student is at the greatest risk of dropping out in the first term or semester of study.

James and Wylie (1970) indicate that 60% of withdrawals took place during the first quarter of the programme South West London College. McIntosh (1972) observed that the dropout rate in the first year of study was approximately 42% of the new enrolment at the British Open University and this was approximately 58.5% of the total number of students who had withdrawn from open university programmes.

Surprisingly there are no studies in India that give any indication of the point or time of dropout of distance learners of any distance and open learning institute. Lakshmi Reddy

(2001) however, reveals that in any academic year during 1988-2000 the percentage of the dropouts, failures and inactive students put together was between 90 and 98. The inactive students are considered to be those who are eligible to appear in term-end examinations (TEE), but did not apply for examination at all. In the case of Dr. B.R. Ambedkar Open University, Andhra Pradesh the average dropout rate during 1993-94 was about 50% (Murali Manohar, 1994, p.77).

From the above studies it can be inferred that the majority of the students have been either dis-enrolled by the institute for their own non-performance or have they dropped out or withdrawn themselves in the first year itself and that too before submission of their first lesson, assignment or any other work. This has happened even prior to completion of the first quarter or prior to their enrolment in the second semester.

Reasons for Dropout

While the time or point of dropout gives an idea as to when to intervene, the reasons for dropout would give an insight into why and how to intervene in preventing or reducing dropout. Though the reasons including the nature and characteristics of dropouts differ from institution to institution and from programme to programme within the same institution they would help in developing or preparing effective packages for curtailing the rate of dropout. The following studies on the reasons for dropout provide sufficient base for policy planners, administrators, teachers and academics at the helm of affairs to think on the problem, to formulate meaningful strategies and to effectively implement them for preventing and/or reducing dropout.

Siquera de Freitas and Lynch (1986) investigated into the reasons for high attrition in an introductory course of National Open University of Venezuela offered to post-secondary students. The reasons for the attrition were: non-utilisation of academic services available in the distance education centres, devotion of less time to study of course materials, simultaneous study of other courses, and perception of course work materials to be more difficult.

Brindleys (1987) studied experiences of 40 randomly selected students of Athabasca University (an open distance education university) that influenced attrition. She identified 13 categories of student experiences touching upon background and defining characteristics such as age and gender; academic variables such as study habits and course availability; environmental variables such as finances, hours of employment, outside engagement and responsibilities; and psychological variables such as perceived utility of studies, satisfaction, goal commitment and stress.

Wilkinson and Sherman (1989) discuss procrastination or the needless postponement of task completion as a reason for student attrition from distance education. Interviews with faculty revealed several interventions, that faculty believed would prevent attrition, including giving students a realistic picture of course/programme demands, providing a structure for progress, reduction of other responsibilities that make priority over coursework, and the recognition of procrastination as a potential negative impact.

Inayat Khan (1989) reports ten reasons for dropout in India. They are: interference of job conditions with study, not getting enough time to complete the course, interference of family/ personal ailment with study, loss of interest in individualised (lone) study, inadequate contact with and advice from teachers, uninteresting instructional/study materials, subsequent admission to a regular college, change in future plans, discouragement caused by non-return of the assignment responses already submitted and absence of timely information on the last date for payment to the institutions. Sahoo (1993) highlighted a variety of reasons for discontinuation of studies by the students enrolled for correspondence courses of Himachal Pradesh University in India. The reasons given by the students are: the course was not job oriented, the course has no link with practical aspects of life, the degree did not command respect in the society, the students were given to understand that the degrees were not recognised by other academic institutions and appointing authorities, difficulties faced in understanding the lessons/scripts, non-availability of suggested references in the library, marked difficulty in understanding the reference materials, untimely supply/availability of lessons/scripts, non-submission of assignments on time, failure to attend personal contact programme(s), lack of library facilities, difficulties in studying without teacher's and classmate's interaction, inability to afford sufficient time for studies, difficulties in completing the courses in given sessions, non-submission of migration certificate, inadequate response from the Directorate of Correspondence Courses to the queries, admission obtained in regular/evening college, permission obtained to appear in examinations through private study, expensive nature of distance education, under achievement in previous semester examinations, personal problems, uninteresting mode of education and physical illness.

In the United States, Camacho Carr, et al (1996) conducted survey on 59 student dropouts and 68 successful graduates (controls) of two year Community-based Nurse-Midwifery Education Programme (CNEP) of Frontier School of Midwifery and Family Nursing (FSMFN) with the purpose of identifying demographic factors, personal and programme characteristics and academic habits that lead to students' success or withdrawal. The findings of the study indicate that despite remarkable similarity in personal characteristics, certain demographic variables, and equal academic achievement at entry into the programme, there were several important differences in their academic habits and how they related to the programme and faculty. The major barriers to completion, as cited by the respondents (sample students), were: family and work responsibilities, financial difficulties, inadequate time parameters for completion of the programme, incompatibility of programme with learning style/needs, problem of starting over as a student, illness or other life event, personality difficulties with preceptors/faculty, and lack of administrative support in the programme.

In the Open University of Hong Kong, Hong Kong 28% of the students on roll did not attend their examinations while 12% of those who appeared in examinations failed (Yuen, et al, 1994). Even in the foundation courses, which have been designed to introduce the students to core elements, significant number of students did not attend their examinations and 11% of those who appeared in the examinations did fail. Further, the rate of non-attendance in examination was one-third higher than the overall OUHK average. In two foundation courses (M111 and M112) of mathematics subject the percentage of initial dropouts (who did not submit any work) was 39.2% and 27.9% of the dropouts respectively. 70% of the dropouts occurred in the first half of presentation (Fan and Chan, 1997, pp.70-80). Level of educational background and lack of experience in distance and open learning were two major causes of student dropout in mathematics foundation courses. Insufficient student commitment, ineffective student support system, inappropriate course material and personal problems such as conflict between study and work were the factors that contributed to high attrition. Age, level of educational background and performance of first tutor marked assignments (TMA-010) were inversely related to the rate of dropout. While sex was not significant in dropout, females seemed to be more persistent. New students generally had higher initial dropout rate (Fan and Chan, op cit.). It makes clear that the students' insufficient preparation, lack of commitment, inappropriate course structure, problems related to course materials, pre-entry educational level and lack of experience in distance and open learning were the reasons for the student dropout.

Boshier (1973) views dropout as a function of the magnitude of the discrepancy among/between the participants' self concept, mis-match between and among students, instructor and instructor, educational processes and environment, including job responsibilities, home responsibilities and so forth.

Eisenberg and Dowsett (1990) studied the influence of some student attributes and achievements in previous open university courses on the dropout rate and achievements in a Technology Project Work Course. They found, from seven years of student results (1982-88), that particular attributes such as occupation affect the dropout rate (trade personnel associated with the electrical, electronic and engineering had a higher percentage dropout than expected), while achievement in the project course appears to be influenced by the student's performance in some various courses such as Introductory Electronics, Control Engineering, Mathematics, and Fundamentals of Computing.

Cleveland-Innes (1994) showed that the initial commitment of students was fragile and did not plan for their studies. According to him commitment was the only useful predictor on dropout decisions and commitment can be influenced by many factors. Kembler's (1989) study proposed a conceptual model which identified the attrition process as a complex interaction of family background, individual attributes, prior educational attainment, goal commitment and institutional commitment as predictor variables

One point of agreement on the phenomenon of attrition is that it is of multivariate nature. The variables posited include the background and circumstances of the individual students (Billings, 1998; Powell, Conway and Ross, 1990), and organisational or institutional variables (DiSilvestro and Markowitz, 1982: Sweet, 1986).

From these studies it is clear that the personal problems, background and characteristics coupled with lack of or reduced commitment from the learner were major reasons for their dropout. The problems and perceptions related to the programme and the institution were rather secondary reasons for their drop out.

Conclusions

From the above overview of the studies carried out on dropouts it can be concluded that:

(i) there is high dropout, withdrawal or attrition at any time/point prior to completion of first lesson or the first quarter of the programme or prior to enrolling in the second semester or before final examination i.e. essentially prior to the completion of the first year itself;

(ii) the reasons are more of personal and less of the programme and institutions;

(iii) the research done is sporadic and unsystematic, particularly in India;

(iv) the research done does not portray or is not adequate to portray any particular trend in dropout of any institution;

(v) the research is either general taking dropout of all the programmes together or is confined, mostly, to one particular programme for a particular year or a cohort at the most;

(vi) the research is not comprehensive in the sense that it does not cover different programmes or all programmes in a particular discipline such as science, arts, engineering, technology, computer, commerce, etc., for any particular academic session or cohort of any one institution or all institutions in a country;

(vii) the research reflects that the definition of dropout varied from study to study. This is because some institutions give final admission to students in one go or at a time, while some other institutions give provisional admission for about six months prior to final enrolment to a programme and certain other specific matters.

(viii) there are no comparative studies comparing dropout rate and reasons across the institutions in a country-between and among dual mode institutions or single mode institutions or between dual mode institutions and single mode institutions;

(ix) the research does not reveal institutional studies of every academic session covering dropouts of all the programmes of the particular institution.

The above overview thus provides good food for thought to the researchers, planners, policy makers and administrators involved with the open and distance education programmes and institutions. Also, it hints at the dire need to give proper direction to the research on dropouts and to institute, encourage and support it so as to make it more comprehensive and systematic.

Before concluding, it would be appropriate to record some of the important suggestions offered by Roberts (1984) based on the theories of Otto Peters, Holmberg and David Sewart about distance education and their implications for early dropout phenomenon. His practical suggestions amongst others for reducing early dropout rates, in brief, include: reduction in number of subjects offered and increase in the number of students enrolled per subject/programme, encouraging more base subjects that have subject content common to several programmes, extension of the life-cycle of a subject to four or even five years without major revision and update, proper and adequate recognition to the academics for their work load in the preparation and trailing of new materials, planned induction procedures for new students, redesigning of assignments and conduct of staff development programmes on assignment marking procedures, making first run of the programme a pilot run and bring out necessary changes based on it, improvement in self-assessment exercises, and appointing counsellors only when there are sufficient number of students enrolled at a particular centre for a programme. Of course, the present day practice in many open and distance education institutions is in tune with the above suggestions. Yet, given the persistent dropout problem, new measures are required to be evolved with regard to the problem in the light of institutional and programme related problems vis-à-vis the nature and characteristics of learners.

Fan and Chan (1997) based on their recent study proposed development / preparation of a package for potential students, enhancement of the existing support system for enrolled students and review of course structure and materials as a package to address the problem of dropout in a comprehensive manner.

These propositions, among others, need to be considered by the distance education policy makers, planners, academics, researchers and administrators while addressing the issues related to the problem of dropout. However, the foremost and important consideration should be to enhance the quality, relevance and timely delivery of course materials to students coupled with effective student support services, including guidance and counselling at different times during their programme of study. These are discussed in the subsequent two chapters.

References

Billings, D.M. (1998). "A conceptual model of correspondence course completion". *The American Journal of Distance Education*, 2(2), 23-35.

Boshier, R. (1973). "Educational participation and dropout: A theoretical model". *Adult Education*. 23, 255-282

Bradt, P. (1956). "Servicemen who take correspondence courses". *Journal of Educational Research*, 50(2), 113-119.

Brindley, J. (1987). *Attrition and completion in distance education: The students' perspective*. Unpublished master's thesis. University of British Columbia, Vancouver B.C. quoted in Camacho Carr, T. et al (1996) cited below.

Camacho Carr, T. et al (1996) "Barriers to completion of a Nurse-Midwifery Distance Education Programme" *Journal of Distance Education*, XI (1), 111-131.

Cleveland - Innes, M. (1994). "Adult student dropout at post-secondary institutions". *The Review of Higher Education*, 17 (4), 423-445.

DiSilvestro, F., and Makowitz, H. (1982). "Contracts and completion rates in correspondence study". *Journal of Educational Research*, 75 (4), 218-221.

Eisenberg, E., and Dowsett, T. (1990). "Student dropout from a distance education project course: A new method of analysis". *Distance Education*,. 11(2), 231-253.

Fan, R.Y.K., and Chan, M.S.C. (1997). "Study on the dropout in mathematics foundation course", *Proceedings of 11th Annual Conference of Asian Association of Open Universities on Quality Assurance in Distance and Open Learning* held from 11-14, 1997 at Kuala Lumpur, Malaysia, 70-80.

Harter, D. (1969). *Why SUNY students fail to complete independent study courses*. State University of New York, New York.

James, B.J., and Wedemeyer, C.A. (1959). "Completion of University correspondence courses by adults". *Journal of Higher Education*. 30 (22), 87-93.

Jones, L.H. and Wylie, A. (1970). "Attrition and achievement in the scheme of private study", *Industrial and Commercial Training*, 2, 8.

Khan, Inayat (1989). "Why students dropout from correspondence courses" in Khan, I. (eds). *Teaching at a Distance*. New Delhi: Amar Publications Pvt. Ltd.

Kember, D. (1989). "A longitudinal process model of dropout from distance education" *Journal of Higher Education*, 60 (3), 278-301.

Lakshmi Redd, M.V. (2001). Learning from the Distance Learners' Behaviour: A case study of Indira Gandhi national Open University. A poster presented at the 20th ICDE World Conference on *The Future of Learning - Learning for the Future: Shaging the Transition* held at Dusseldorf, Germany from 01-05, April, 2001.

McIntosh, N.E. (1972), *Research for a new institution*. Milton Keynes. United Kingdom Open University.

Murali Manohar, K. (1994). *Distance education: Studies in quality and quantitative aspects*, Warangal: Indian Distance Education Association, p. 77.

Peters, O. (1992). "Some observation on dropping out in distance education". *Distance Education*, 13 (2), 234-269.

Powell, R., Conway, C., and Ross, L. (1990). "Effects of student predisposing characteristics on student success". *Journal of Distance Education*. V (1), 5-19.

Roberts, D.W. (1980). *An analysis of the dropout from external study programmes at Goulburn CAE. 1975-80.* Unpublished Master thesis, quoted in Roberts, D. (1984) cited below.

Roberts, D. (1984). "Ways and means of reducing early student dropout rates". *Distance Education*, 5(1), 50-71.

Sahoo, P.K. (1993). *Higher education at a distance*. Delhi: Sanchar Publishers.

Sheath, H.C. (1965). *External studies - the first 10 years*. Armidale, N.S.W: University of New England quoted in Roberts, D. (1984) op. Cit.

Siquera de Freitas, K and Lynch, P. (1986). "Factors affecting student success at the National Open University of Venezuela" *Distance Education*. 7(2), 191-200.

Sweet, R. (1986). "Student dropout in distance education: An application of Tinto's model". *Distance Education*, 7(2), 201-213.

Wilkinson, T. and Sherman, T. (1989). "Distance education and student procrastination". *Educational Technology*, 29(12), 24-27, quoted in Camacho Carr, T., et al (1996), op. Cit.

Yuen, K., Siaw, I., Hing, G., and Hatchard, D. (1994). "A Study on the dropout of Hong Kong's distance learners". *Proceedings of the Conference on Distance Education: Windows on the Future.* New Zealand: The Correspondence School, 512-519.

5

Quantity and Quality Considerations for Effective Delivery of Student Support Services

With a humble beginning made about four decades ago, in the form of correspondence education through correspondence institutes established in till then single mode conventional Universities, distance education in India has become popular with establishment of independent single mode distance education institutions such as Open Universities, Open Schools, etc. As stated in the previous section, there are now 10 Open Universities, 62 Directorates/Institutes of Correspondence / Distance Education amongst many other institutions offering distance education. Thus, the efforts for development of distance education have not only metamorphosed the single mode conventional institutions/Universities into dual mode ones but also led to the establishment of statutory, autonomous, single mode distance and open education institutions/ Universities.

There has been increasing recognition of distance and open education as an effective means to provide mass(ive) and democratic education to all the needy and deprived sections of the society. The nature of distance and open education has led to innovative and complex organisational structure at the institutional level and multiplicity of collaborations with other institutions, both educational and non-educational, time and again. The collaborations continued to multiply and organizational structure became more complex because of continuing increase in the number of programmes, the student enrolment, the diversity of programmes, the variety of learning experiences, the services to be provided to the learners and the variety of assessment and evaluation procedures. All these have, no doubt, contributed to the growth of distance education in leaps and bounds (Lakshmi Reddy, 1996). This, however, reflects only the quantitative growth of distance and open education.

At the same time the quality of distance education cannot be ignored. It is, perhaps, true when Ramanujam (1995) says: " The weakness of the distance mode, on the other hand, cannot be ignored or glossed over. The problems of supplying up-to-date knowledge to students and the difficulties in giving and getting instant feedback do worry the academics who want to give the best to their students in the best possible manner". Added to this, the quality of distance education in terms of delivery of programmes to the learners remained poor and the students are demotivated. This can be inferred from high rate of dropout, withdrawal and attrition in distance and open learning institutions, as noticed in the previous chapter. Nevertheless, the quality of distance education is visible in the multimedia package of learning materials produced by these institutions. But, the untimely production of these materials, their distribution to the students and provision of improper support services to them are the admitted failures, of course, off the records in delivery of the programmes. Only one thing which is not coming out on record or is not being made public or which cannot be understood easily is the nightmare of experiences, problems and difficulties the distance learners face in completing the programme for which they are enrolled. Thus, the major problems of quality of distance education centre around the delivery of programmes to the learners. These problems and issues related to quality of distance education need to be carefully identified and considered while taking decisions on expanding distance education.

Purpose

In order to ensure the quality of distance education programmes the efforts for development and establishment of support services for a programme should start sufficiently in advance of launching the programme. Prior to launching of a programme the distance education institution should take stock of the existing workload on the existing staff involved in the delivery of different programmes currently on offer and review the workload and assess additional staff requirement. Otherwise, the quality of support services will reamin poor and this would result in unnecessary hardships to the students on the one hand and loss of credibility of the very system on the other. Therefore, if the quality of a programme should not be sacrificed for the quantity of the programme or vice-versa the need for establishment of proper delivery mechanism to provide quality support services should not be undermined.

In this chapter, an attempt is made to identify the quantitative and qualitative aspects and issues of distance education programme vis-à-vis student support services which are very important in effective delivery of programmes. While identifying different issues and their aspects the programmes with or without practical components such as lab work, field work, project work, work experiences, computer exposure and other kinds of experience have been thoroughly looked into. The issues identified are, also not exhaustive, but suggestive and provide a broad frame work—quantitative and qualitative—that can work as a guide for development and delivery of effective student support services. These issues would help in promoting and maintaining the quality of distance education programme as a whole.

Student Support Services: Quantity and Quality Considerations

Any distance education programme should be launched only when all necessary arrangements or preparations for launching it have been thoroughly completed. These preparations should, in fact, start well ahead of launching of the programme. However, there is no hard and fast rule as to how advance the preparatory efforts should start. But the earliest is the best. This all depends on the nature of the programme (presence or absence of practical components, etc.), objectives of the programme, geographical coverage of the programme, nature, quality and quantity of support structures/system required and so on. In other words, the period of advance preparations for development and establishment of support services vary from programme to programme, But, it is undisputed that the programmes with practical component require relatively longer period for making arrangements or for establishing the required support service system. Effective support services to the students can be ensured only when the preparations for launching of a programme are over and well done before launching of the programme. All efforts related to development and establishment of support system for providing effective support services to students fall under the following three categories.

(i) Pre-programme Launching Stage;
(ii) Programme Launching Stage; and
(iii) Programme Delivery Stage.

The efforts under each of these stages are, however, not compartmentalised and the efforts of developing and/delivery of student support services in the preceding stage form a basis for efforts in immediately succeeding stage. The efforts at each stage should always be aimed at addressing the issues of support services that may pertain to the succeeding stage. However, the issues identified under each stage may not be exhaustive and there may be more issues that can still be identified. Also, these may vary from programme to programme depending on the nature, area of coverage and objectives of the programme. The different issues identified under each stage and related aspects are discussed below.

I. Pre-programme Launching Stage

This is an important stage requiring careful conception and identification of different aspects of the issues involved for initiating the efforts of establishing an effective student support services system. Thoroughly thought out and well conceived preparatory efforts would pave a long way in establishing a meaningful and adequate support services system. All important aspects and issues that have bearing on development and establishment of effective delivery mechanism should, therefore, be taken into consideration at this stage itself because an effective support system determines the success of programme delivery. The important issues and their qualitative and quantitative aspects that need consideration at this stage are shown in Table 5.1.

The consideration of the quantitative and qualitative aspects of the above issues would help in putting effective efforts for establishment of support service system. Also, these would form a basis for preparations to be made under the programme launching stage or programme readiness stage.

II. Programme Launching/Readiness Stage

After identifying different issues and their qualitative and quantitative aspects related to establishment of student support system/structure the crucial tasks that follow pertain to completion of the task of establishing (a) necessary support system/structure and (b) completion of preparation and development of all materials necessary for launching the programme. This requires identification of different issues and aspects related to launching of the programme and are shown in Table 5.2.

It is essential to keep all these issues involved and their aspects in view and address them effectively and adequately. Only then it is possible to be ready for launching the programme. The efficiency of delivery of the programmes depends upon the degree of readiness at the time of launching of the programme. The higher the degree of readiness the higher would be the efficiency of delivery of the programme. Thus, the extent of readiness at the time of launching of the

Table 5.1: Issues and Aspects Related to Pre-programme Launching Stage

Sl. No.	*Issues*	*Quantitative Aspect*	*Qualitative Aspect*
1.	Target Population	• Rough estimate of the potential students available for the programme: • in initial years • in subsequent years	• An idea of profile—background, qualifications, experience, etc.
		• Minimum No. of students required for the programme viability • Maximum No. of students that the programme can cover • Optimum No. of students for effective delivery of the programme	• Cost analysis of the programme
		• Geographical distribution of students • Expected No. of students for the launching year • No. of students to be admitted in the first year	• Determining factors of access • Proper estimate • Identification of qualifications, experience, etc. required to be fixed for admission.
2.	Status of course materials	• The No. of courses or blocks: • Developed, • Under preparation and , development. • No. of audio-video tapes developed and under preparation. • Time required for preparation, completion and development of the remaining courses/tapes	• Checking the mistakes, ascertaining the corrections through corrigenda to ensure quality • Comprehensiveness of coverage and quality • Ascertaining the stage of preparation of the courses/tapes under preparation • Ascertaining the extent of content covered and to be covered • Thorough planning for timely completion of the pending tasks

3.	Programme details	• Size of the structure, time required for development • Programme fees (amount) • Eligibility criteria for admission to the programme	• Brief description of the nature of Structure and Services. • Affordability by the students • Relevance of age, educational qualifications, experience, etc.
4.	Student support system/ structures required	• No. of institutions to be established as: • Study centres • Programme centres • Work centres • Other centres • Possible mutual benefits: • Financial • Non-financial • Others, if any • Ways/procedures of identifying the best institutions and approaching them • Minimum, optimum and maximum number of students per centre	• Nature of institutions suitable for the programme • Infrastructure and staff required to be available with these institutions • List of suggested institutions and their location • Possible problems, difficulties, losses, if any and ways overcoming them • Exchange of suitable materials and information • Effective human interaction • Development of appropriate formats, if any, required for obtaining relevant information • Methods/procedures of contract and its termination • Cost-benefit or expenditure-income details of the offer
5.	Timing the launch of the programme	• Possible date of advertisement • Formats of advertisement • Publicity	• Payment norms • Media to be used • Variety and flexibility in the formats • Different ways/means of publicity

Table 5.2 Issues and Aspects Related to Programme Launching Stage

Sl. No.	*Issues*	*Quantitative Aspect*	*Qualitative Aspect*
1.	Student support Structure	• No. of established • Study Centres • Programme Centres • Work Centres • Other Centres, if any, with complete address, etc.	• Brief description of various aspects, functions etc., of centres and their functionaries. • Corrigenda, if any • Adequacy of the structure
2.	Course Materials	• Availability of completely developed • Self-instructional materials • A.V. Cassettes • Manuals • Other related materials	• Extent/degree of readiness, in case all the materials are not ready • Determine the time frame for development vis-à-vis the programme delivery schedule.
3.	Prospectus and Applications, Student Handbook, Programme guide, Resource Persons' Handbooks, Manuals, etc.	• Number expected and available • Despatch to different centres • Receipt by all centers well in advance.	• Adequacy of materials • Corrigenda, if any • Ascertaining the receipt of Prospectus and Applications by all centres before the advertisement appears.
4.	Advertisement	• Release of the advertisement on the scheduled date	• Appearance in the pre-selected newspaper(s) • Clarity and attractiveness • Corrigenda, if any, in time

5.	Admission/ Registration of students	• No. of applications already available at relevant places/centres • No. of extra applications received • No. of applications sold • Balance remaining • No. of filled-in applications received from the students • No. of applications scrutinised, rejected and accepted • No. of students admitted • Finalisation of admission	• Programme-wise details • Methods by which sold-by post, by hand, etc. • Timely despatch, if by post • Detailed periodical sales account • Timely admission. • Settlement of discrepancies, if any • Setting proper deadlines for supplementary list • Reasonable extension of deadline, if necessary • Accurate list of admitted students

Table 5.3 Issues and Aspects Related to Programme Delivery Stage.

Sl. No.	Issues	Quantitative Aspect	Qualitative Aspect
1.	Address labels	• Addresses of all students of all programmes • No. of labels of each student	• Clarity of print of labels • Correctness of the address • Corrections, if any, to be carried out on the labels • Timely development of labels of supplementary list • Timely supply of labels to Materials Distribution Division/Unit concerned

2.	Material distribution	• Despatch of SIMs, assignments, etc., to
		  • Regional Centres concerned
		  • Study Centres concerned
		  • Students concerned
		• Delay in despatch
			• Timely despatch as per schedule
			• Identification of courses for which despatch is not done or delayed
			• Timely intimation to students on delay
			• Allowance of reasonable time to students to adjust to schedule of operations.

3.	Assignments Evaluation	• Number prescribed for each course • Number of assignments expected based on enrolment • Number of assignments actually received • Extension of deadline/dates for submission • Number of TMAs, CMAs, FAs, etc. • Number submitted or received in time	• Number evaluated in prescribed time • Timely payment to Academic Counsellors • Reasons, if any, for low turnout of assignments • Evaluation and feedback as per guidelines • Timely feedback to students

4.	Counselling Sessions	• Number of sessions:
		  • Prescribed for each course/programme
		  • Scheduled
			• Advance communication of schedule of counselling to students
			• Adequate use of cassettes available

		• Held as per schedule • Which used audio cassettes only • Which used video cassettes only • Which used both A & V cassettes	• Counselling as per guidelines • Timely payment to Academic Counsellors
5.	Practicals - Lab/ computer / field/project work, etc.,	• Number of centres established for providing: • Lab work • Computer work • Field work • Other work experiences • Availability of infrastructure facilities • Availability of Staff • Availability of materials • Period or duration of exposure	• Availability of: • Suitable infrastructure • Adequate qualified and trained staff • Sufficient materials of quality • Convenience of practical location to students • Duration and timings of work
6.	Examinations, evaluation and results	• Availability of exam application forms • Advanced publication of the dates • For submission of applications • Of examinations for different courses/ programmes • Of release/publication of results • For despatch of marks statements, certificates, etc.	• Adequacy and timely supply • Advance communication • Proper publicity • Method/media to be used • Mode of supply of forms • Clarity of grades in certificates • Timely despatch of certificates, degrees

programme determines the success of delivery of the programme. Therefore, all the issues and aspecs related to the programme launching stage need to be addressed effectively for effective programme delivery.

III. Programme Delivery Stage

This is an important stage which raises lot many issues that will have operational implications for both the administration and the students. The provision of support services to the students depends on the adequacy and quality of the support system. The successful delivery of the programme is dependent upon well planned schedule of operations, strict adherence to the schedule of operations and efficiency of co-ordination of different operations. All the issues related to various operations during this stage need utmost attention for effective provision of support services to students. The important issues and their quantitative and qualitative aspects that require thorough consideration at this stage are shown in Table 5.3.

The different operations during this stage form a chain. Each operation, in fact, has a link with the other and any problem or delay in one operation shows its impact on the other to follow. Therefore, clear delineation and demarcation of operations to different functionaries or authorities is very essential. Otherwise, there is a possibility of undermining the responsibility by neglecting the significance of operations and seeking excuses in the work of others involved in similar or related operations. In the process there would be an overlap in the operations or break in the chain of operations and as a sequel to it the provision of services to the students and the efficiency of programme delivery would be hampered. Therfore, all the issues and aspects of operations during the programme delivery stage require meticulous consideration and co-ordination for effective delivery of programme.

Furthermore, different quantitative and qualitative aspects of the issues under the above three stages are inter-linked in the sense that some of the issues and aspects of second stage have their grounding in those of the first stage and those of third stage have their grounding in those of second stage. It means addressing the issues in the successive stage requires their consideration in the preceding stage as well. Therefore, in order to strike a balance between the quantitative and qualitative promotion of distance education programme, particularly in providing effective support services and maintenance of standards, there is a need for exhaustive, elaborate and comprehensive identification of all possible issues and their aspects and for addressing them by developing well co-ordinated, tight and strict schedule of operations at all the above three stages of the programme.

References

Lakshmi Reddy, M.V. (1996). *"Action and Feedback Research in Distance Education: Some Priority Areas", Paper presented at the Professor G. Ram Reddy Memorial Seminar on Research in Distance Education in India* held at Hyderabad on 23rd November, 1996, (p.1).

Ramanujam, P.R. (1995). *Reflections on Distance Education for India*, Jaipur: Manak Publications (P) Limited, p.39.

6

A Scientific Approach to Organising Counselling for Distance Learners

Distance education is a gift of technology to the world. It is the technology which has helped distance education to establish itself as a viable supplement, complement and alternative, to the conventional system of education. The literature on distance education unequivocally emphasises the need and significance of support services to the distance learners. In chapter 5 we have looked at different issues that require thorough consideration while establishing student support services system for effective delivery of distance education programme. Nevertheless, the inherent problems associated with the system such as the distance between the teacher and the learner, the isolation of learner from the institute and the absence of chances for regular interaction with colleagues, student friends and teachers will occasionally force the distance learner feel the need for counselling through face-to-face contact. Counselling is a part of specified support services provided to the distance learners. In this chapter an attempt is made to evolve a scientific approach to organising counselling for distance learners.

There is no conclusive proof to prove the necessity of face-to-face elements in distance education or to reject them as conventional embellishments (Holmberg, 1985).

Notwithstanding the extreme argument that face-to-face contact in the form of counselling between the distance teacher and the taught is against the concept of distance education, the need for counselling to the distance learners cannot be undermined. This looks obvious when we look at the characteristics of the distance learners, the distance education institutions and the learning process (IGNOU, 1993).

The learner characteristics primarily include:

— Isolation from the co-learners, the teacher, and the institution;
— The experiences in different walks of life;
— The attitudes, opinions, etc., may be positive or negative, formed towards certain things, persons, institutions, etc.;
— The commitments to their family and their office work;
— The time constraints;
— The heterogeneity in terms of age, marital, economic and social status, geographical location; and
— The background and experience, both educational and occupational.

The characteristics of the institution include:

— Distance location of the institution, though relatively less remote regional and study centres do exist at different places;
— Complex structure of the institution;
— The problems of coordination and delivery of services;

The characteristics of learning process include:

— Learner-centred approach to learning;
— Multiple learning strategies/muti-media package;
— Variety of study skills for learning.

In order to fill all the gaps that arise due to all or any of the above characteristics of the learner, the institution and/or the learning process there is an inevitable need for providing counselling services to students. Of course, the Self-instructional Materials (SIMs) are supposed to be self-sufficient in promoting self-learning. However, SIMs cannot be equally effective with all the learners of all the programmes. Hence, the need for counselling to meet the individual differences, difficulties and problems in learning.

The basic purpose of advocating support services to the distance learners is to provide for certain gaps which the distance teacher, the institution and the teaching-learning materials (multi-media package) are unable to or cannot provide. As Ramanujam (1995) rightly points out "The effectiveness of student support services does not depend merely on its formal structure. The educational value of the services that a student gets must be taken as the ultimate criterion to judge the validity of the services offered". Counselling is one of the important components of student support services in distance education which enables the distance learners pursue their course smoothly and effectively by providing for their felt needs, gaps, problems and difficulties that otherwise would lead to serious consequences such as stagnation, drop out and wastage. However, face-to-face teaching or counselling is an extra component having the following five main functions (IGNOU, 1993).

- *(i)* Developing among the learners the study skills that they need to possess for studying at a distance;
- *(ii)* Dealing with problems and difficulties encountered by the learners in understanding the subject matter and in pursuing the courses/programmes;
- *(iii)* Providing practical work or guidance on other assignments such as project work, workshops, etc.;
- *(iv)* Teaching the learners methods and techniques of learning from each other; and
- *(v)* Training the learners in individualised learning.

Present Institutional Practice of Counselling in Distance Education: A Brief Critique on IGNOU Practice.

Present practice in distance education, particularly in open universities in India is that the *number* of counselling sessions or personal contact programmes per course or programme is decided at the Headquarters by the concerned faculty. Some counselling sessions or contact programmes for some courses or programmes are compulsory while other sessions or contact programmes are not compulsory. By scanning the counselling schedules received from different study centres of IGNOU in respect of different programmes over a period of 3 academic years (1993-95) the author observed that the counselling schedules were prepared by Coordinators of the study centres and were sent to the learners and the counsellors concerned. There is no role for the learners and counsellors in deciding these schedules. Further, the schedule is prepared at a time for a period ranging from one to three months covering different blocks of different courses of different programmes specifying the place, date, time and period of counselling. This means that both the learner (counsellee) and the counsellor are either ignored or totally out of scene in deciding the topic, place, date, time, period and frequency of counselling sessions of any course or programme.

By looking at the response to such counselling schedules one gets a discouraging picture. For instance, the average attendance of students of IGNOU in 1993 in the case of Diploma in Operations Management (DOM) was 6.7% of total enrolment in the programme. In the case of Diploma in Human Resources Development (DHRM), Diploma in Marketing Management (DMM), Diploma in Financial Management (DFM), B.Sc., and Bachelor's Degree Programme (BDP-BA and B.Com.) it was 11.92%, 12.09%, 12.39%, 13.33% and 13.97% respectively. Surprisingly, in the case of Computer Programmes too, where much practical work was involved, the response was 49.8% only (Lakshmi Reddy, 1995). Regarding the personal contact programmes (PCPs) of correspondence education in India, Dutt (1989) observes that face-to-face teaching is overemphasised during PCPs while Rathore (1995) finds that sufficient time is not given to students to discuss their academic problems. Yet the scheduling of the counselling sessions or contact programmes irrespective of the learners' demand , need and attendance is going on leading to wastage and even misuse of funds. It shows that the past experience in counselling, lack of demand from and interest among learners, wastage of resources are being ignored outright in organising counselling to distance learners.

Focus in Counselling of Distance Learners

Counselling, a provision for face-to-face contact, is perhaps, a vanishing point in distance education. However, it acquires its real meaning only when it addresses the real needs, problems, difficulties, etc., faced by the learners at different stages of different learning experiences in pursuing their programme of study. Also, it should help to reconcile the conflicting demands of home, work, learning and education. Organising counselling to distance learners should be done in tune with the intended purpose and philosophy underlying the student support services. Otherwise, counselling would turn into a necessary evil, and the very purpose of it would be defeated It would even lead to erosion of the meaning or the concept of distance education itself. In addition to this, a large chunk of financial resources would go waste as there would be insignificant percentage of student attendance.

Scientific Approach to Organising Counselling

Counselling for distance learners should take into account different aspects, issues and factors which have direct and indirect bearing on the distance learners. The scientific approach to organising counselling to distance learners can be presented and discussed under four heads viz.,

(i) the basic assumptions related to organising counselling;

(*ii*) the aspects, stages and issues related to programme pursuance by the learners;

(*iii*) the ground work the organisers/academics at different levels should do; and

(*iv*) the steps involved in scientific approach to organising counselling for distance learners.

(i) Basic Assumptions related to Organising Counselling

There are certain basic assumptions that should be kept in view while organising counselling for distance learners. They are:

1. Counselling schedules prepared at Study Centres should not take the shape of classroom time-table of conventional institutions;
2. Counselling topics should emerge out of identified/selected felt/real needs, problems, difficulties, etc. of the learners;
3. Learner-centred approach should be followed rather than Coordinator or Counsellor centred approach;
4. Counselling should use multi-media approach wherever possible;
5. Counselling activity should not be confined to study centres alone and should be done at different levels by different academics of the system;
6. Counselling should not turn into class room teaching-learning situation.

The above assumptions are slightly elaborated below.

1. Counselling schedules prepared at the Study Centres should not take the shape of classroom time-table of conventional institutions.

Scheduling of counselling should emerge out of the counsellee-learners' demand for it rather than allowing it to be done according to the convenience of the Coordinators of study centres who are deciding the counselling schedules unilaterally. It should, in fact, be decided by the Coordinators in consultation with and as per convenience of the counsellor as well as the learners concerned.

2. *Counselling topic should emerge out of identified/ selected felt/real needs, problems, etc. of the learners.*

The topic of counselling should not be decided by the Coordinators of study centres by taking course, block or unit titles as presented in the SIMs. The topics should be selected keeping in view the felt needs, problems, difficulties of the learners as communicated by them to the counsellor or as perceived by him based on his interaction with different students of a particular course or programme.

3. *Learner-centred approach should be followed rather than Coordinator or Counsellor- centred approach.*

The focal element in counselling should be the learners (counsellees). So every activity related to organisation of counselling should centre around the learners only.

4. *Counselling should use multi-media approach wherever possible.*

Instead of resorting to only face-to-face counselling at once the materials available in different media that address specific needs, problems, difficulties, etc., should be explored, used and exhausted first. Only then it would be more meaningful and in tune with muti-media approach in distance education.

5. *Counselling should be done at different levels by different academics of the system.*

Counselling activity should not be confined to study centres only. It is necessary to organise counselling at all levels—Headquarters, Regional Centre and Study Centres. These levels should vary depending upon the need, urgency, nature, magnitude, quality and quantity of the counselling services required by the distance learners of different programmes of different nature, size and area of coverage.

6. *Counselling should not turn into a class room teaching-learning situation.*

The process of counselling should be in the form of need-based, problem solving, difficulty-redressing interaction and service leading to remedy or resolution of the felt needs, problems and difficulties of counsellee-learner rather than monotonous one way dumping of information already available in SIMs.

(ii) The Aspects, Stages and Issues Related to Programme Pursuance by Learners.

The needs, problems and difficulties of distance learners relate to the following aspects or areas:

— Study skills;
— Institutional arrangements;
— Orientation to study at a distance;
— Preparing assignment responses, Project Proposals, Reports, etc.;
— Appearing in the examinations.

Once the learner gets admission into a programme (s)he starts identifying and feeling the need for various things and faces different problems, difficulties and barriers at different stages in fulfilling the needs. The specific stages and possible needs, problems and difficulties, in brief, can be as follows.

After admission and prior to receipt of material:

— When the material would be sent to the learner?
— In how many despatches and for which courses?
— If there is any delay in dispatching the material, the reasons thereof and the revised schedule of the despatch etc.

After receipt of the SIMs and during submission of the assignments:

— Non-receipt of certain material or partial receipt of materials,
— Receipt of irrelevant material or material in wrong medium,
— Non-receipt of assignments and related cards, etc.,
— Laxity or gaps in information/materials received,
— Any doubts on assignments submission.

After submitting the assignment responses and till the receipt of proper grade sheet:

— Delay in receipt of evaluated assignments and grade sheet,
— Reasons for delay in receipt of the evaluated assignments and the grade sheets,
— Getting the mistakes, errors, etc., if any, rectified in the grade sheets.

Before, during and after taking up the practicals:

— Fulfilling the requisite conditions,
— Preparing for the practicals,
— Starting, doing and finishing the practicals in the lab, etc.

Before, during and after the submission of project work or other assigned work:

— Format and procedure of submitting the proposal,
— Details on submission of synopsis, report, dissertation, etc.

At the time of submission of examination application form:

— Where to get the application form?
— What is the last date for submission of the form?
— Whom to submit the form?
— What are the details, if any, of submitting applications with fine?

While preparing for the examinations:

— Tips for the examination,
— Getting previous question papers or model question papers for a new programme.

Counselling the students on their needs, problems and difficulties is very important at two points—decision point or some kind of barrier (IGNOU, 1993). Some of the important decision points and barriers may be relating to:

Whether to withdraw from the course/programme or keep going?

— Clarifying reasons,
— Explaining the frustration and disappointment,
— Showing alternative course of action,
— Encouraging to return.

Whether to miss an assignment or not?

— What is the consequence of missing certain compulsory assignment or activity of the course or programme?

How to tailor the time for:

— The family?
— The job?
— The course/programme?

How to go about studying the SIMs and doing the assignments, the practicals and the project work?

— Adaptation,
— Study methods and techniques,
— Note making methods and techniques.
— What are the best ways and means of approaching the examinations? And so on.

The organisers of counselling should have the knowledge of organizing counselling and about different aspects, stages and issues related to programme being pursued by the learners. Such knowledge would help them in identifying the specific issues and aspects related to different levels of learners' progress. This would also help in grouping the learners based on the issues that require counselling.

(iii) Ground Work the Organisers/Academics at Different Levels Should Do

The organisers/academics should understand the learners, their programmes of studies, the multi-media package available, the rules, regulations, and arrangements of the organisation, the resources and facilities available at the study centers and regional centres to which they are attached and so on. In brief, they should have a bird's eye view of the following :

(a) The Learners

- — Their number and nature,
- — Their socio-economic background such as age, marital status, education, occupation, experience, etc..
- — Distance between the study centre and the residence of the learners
- — Their felt needs, problems, difficulties, etc. common to all students, specific to certain students of particular course(s) or of particular socio-economic group,
- — Their domestic, career related, work related, financial and health related problems including any physical disability, marital break down, childcare, unemployment/reemployment,
- — Their demand for counselling
- — The time and dates convenient for their counselling,
- — Finding, adjusting, restructuring and prioritising of their time,
- — Their busy, moderate and less work days and months of the year

(b) The programme

- — Its nature—whether science, arts, engineering, technology, etc.,
- — The normal difficulty level of its course content as perceived by learners and faculty concerned.
- — The specific topics of different courses of the programme which are generally considered to be

difficult by the faculty of the School, the learners and counsellors,

— The content load of the programme.

(c) *The Multi-media package*

— Whether the SIMs and other materials have been sent to and received by the students and counsellors,
— The availability of audio-video cassettes' at different centres
— The schedules of radio broadcasts, telecasts, teleconferences, etc.,
— The chart or list of the content/topics covered under different media,
— Different kinds of printed information which can substitute or ease the counselling burden,
— The quality, cost, etc., of audio-video cassettes.

(d) *The rules, regulations and arrangements of the organisation relating to:*

— Change of student address, Study Centre, Regional Centre, course, programme, etc.,
— Mailing delays, possible systems breakdown and remedies therefore, etc.,
— Evaluation of assignments, project reports, etc.
— Conduct of counselling sessions, ECPs, practicals, examinations, etc.

(e) *The Study Centre*

— The availability of multi-media package,
— The availability of sufficient accommodation,
— The availability of equipments, T.V., V.C.R., etc. and other facilities,
— The availability of trained academic counsellors in general and their availability on the scheduled dates,
— Standby arrangement of the academic counsellors, if required, and

— The willingness/acceptance of academic counsellors to take up counselling on the scheduled dates.

The role of Regional Centres and the Headquarters is paramount in facilitating the organisation of counselling particularly at the study centres. The role should be to:

— Ensure that the SIMs and other materials reach all the students and different centres sufficiently in advance,
— Provide multi-media package, equipments, TV., VCR/VCP, tape recorder, etc. to study centres,
— Appoint sufficient number of academic counsellors and provide sufficient infrastructure, material, training and manpower,
— Provide information about learners' background i.e. complete profile of learners attached to the study centres.

The above ground work, if done properly, would enable the counsellors and the organisers/academics (at the study centre or at any place of counselling) understand thoroughly the learners, the programmes they are pursuing, the multi-media package and the facilities available at the study centre or the place of counselling. The facilitative efforts by Regional Centres and Headquarters would further add to it.

(iv) Steps involved in Scientific Approach to Organising Counselling

The scientific basis for organising counselling should be the distance learners' profile, their felt needs, problems, difficulties, etc. This scientific base is possible only when there is systematic approach to assessing of their needs, problems and difficulties and to the whole issue of organising counselling to distance learners. There are several steps involved in scientific approach to organising counselling and are as follows:

1. ***Identify the needs, problems, difficulties etc. of learners which require counselling.***

Under this step the important question that matters is whether there is any demand from students for counselling? If the answer to the question is in affirmative then only the question of identification of the needs, problems, difficulties, etc. expressed by them arise. These may be related to materials, course options, reregistration, change of courses, programme, address, Study Centre or Regional Centre, assignments, practicals, project work, examinations, or any other general information. The learners, needs, problems, difficulties, etc., related to the above matters should be invited from them at different time periods. It does not, of course, require development of any research tool nor conduct of a study on these matters. Letters received from students now and then are enough to complete the task identifying their needs, problems, difficulties, etc.

2. ***Analyse the identified needs, problems, difficulties, etc., of learners***

Once the needs, problems, difficulties etc. of the learners are identified then follows the question—"What are the main areas, aspects under which these needs, problems, difficulties, issues, etc. fall?" This requires analysis and classification of these needs, problems, difficulties, etc. into different categories based on different criteria. Here, again one need not think of applying statistical techniques to do this. Simple sorting of letters or recording of oral requests of learners into different categories based on frequency or similarity of needs, problems, difficulties, etc., would be sufficient.

3. ***Prioritise and select the needs, problems, difficulties, etc. of learners that really require counselling.***

After analysing and classifying the needs, problems, difficulties, etc. they need to be prioritised in each class keeping in view the urgency, intensity, and approximate duration of time required for counselling the learners. After prioritisation, these are to be divided into groups on the basis of the place suitable for organising counselling i.e. whether at the Headquarters (may be through teleconferencing by the School or Division concerned) or at the Regional Centre or at the Study Centre. This grouping should be done at Study Centre level and the priority list should be sent to the respective places for appropriate counselling.

4. ***Identify different men, media, materials, methods and techniques relevant to provision of counselling on the selected needs, problems, difficulties, etc. of the learners.***

Here comes the questions of—Who are the right personnel to be involved for the purpose of organising counselling at different places? What should be the basis for involvement of the part-time faculty available at the study centers, the full-time faculty at the Regional Centre or at the Headquarters or any other faculty outside the University who may be specially identified? What are the special criteria, if any, to be followed in deciding upon the people to be involved in counselling at different levels?

Next comes the question of the suitability of means, materials and/or modes of organising counselling? Whether it is:

- face-to-face counselling? If so, should it be
  - — individual to individual? or
  - — individual to group? or
  - — group to group?
- through writing? If so, is it through
  - — letters? or
  - — handbooks? or
  - — leaflets? or
  - — brochures? or
  - — any other relevant printed material already available?
- though telephone? If so, is it through
  - — one-to-one? or
  - — teleconferencing? or
  - — answerphone?

- through cassettes? If so, is it through
  - — audio cassettes? or
  - — video cassettes? or
  - — both?
- through broadcast, telecast, or teleconference or videoconference?
- through computer-based interactive video disc, etc.? or
- through any other specially developed means, techniques, and/or materials?

5. ***Analyse the men, media, materials, methods and techniques identified under the step 4 above in view of the needs, problems, difficulties prioritised under step 3 above.***

The men, materials, media, methods and techniques should be analysed and classified into different groups vis-à-vis needs, problems, difficulties, etc., of the learners and their suitability in addressing the same.

6. ***Prioritise and select only the suitable men/counsellors, media, materials, methods and techniques for counselling.***

After analysing and classifying men/counsellors, media, materials, methods and techniques they should be prioritised and only the suitable or more appropriate ones be selected in the light of the nature, magnitude, urgency, and intensity of the needs, problems, difficulties, etc. of the learners.

7. ***Organise counselling to the learners.***

Finally, counselling should be organized by the selected persons in the appropriate mode by utilising different materials, media, methods and techniques suitable to different categories of learners and also depending upon the nature and magnitude of their needs, problems and difficulties. In spite of all the efforts, ensuring smooth and effective conduct of counselling, at times, becomes difficult.

To avoid certain practical difficulties in organising counselling, it is always better to ensure:

- — the willingness/acceptance of the counsellors to provide counselling on the selected dates and topics;
- — the convenience of timings for both learners and counsellors;
- — the alternative arrangement and solutions, if any, available that can be utilized in case of any exigency; and
- — availability of the necessary support staff, materials, accommodation, money, equipment, etc. at the centres of counselling.

Counselling in distance education, therefore, should be organized, as stated earlier, in tune with the intended purpose and underlying philosophy and by taking into cognizance the real and felt needs, problems, difficulties, etc., of learners, the convenience of counsellor and the financial implications in providing infrastructural facilities. The steps involved in scientific approach to organising counselling which are discussed in this chapter would be of great help in this regard.

To conclude, counselling acquires its real meaning, serves the intended purpose, prevents wastage and misuse of human, monetary, and material resources and also saves the time and energy of different personnel and learners involved only when the counselling is organised by approaching it scientifically. Otherwise it (counselling) would remain an ornamental adage to the system of distance education.

References

Dutt, R. (1989). "Developing of Correspondence Courses in India - A Survey-cum-stocking", in I.Khan (ed). *Teaching at a Distance,* Delhi: Amar Prakashan.

Holmberg, B. (1985). Status and Trends in Distance Education, Lector Publishing, Lund, quoted in H.C.S. Rathore (1995), "Personal Contact Programmes of Correspondence Institutes in India: An evaluation", *Indian Journal of Open Learning*, Vol. 4, No. 1, pp.5-21.

IGNOU (1993) "Counselling" Block 3 of DE-4 *Student Support Services*, New Delhi: Division of Distance Education, Indira Gandhi National Open University.

Lakshmi Reddy, M.V. (1995). *Consolidated Report of Counselling Feedback Reports of the Year 1993*, New Delhi: Regional Services Division, Indira Gandhi National Open University (unpublished), p.65.

Ramanujam, P.R. (1995). *Reflections on Distance Education for India*, New Delhi: Manak Publications Pvt. Ltd, p.68.

Rathore, H.C.S. (1995). "Personal Contact Programmes of Correspondence Institutes in India: An Evaluation", *Indian Journal of Open Learning*. Vol;. 4, No. 1, pp.15-21

7

Action and Feedback Research in Distance Education: Some Priority Areas

Development of distance education in India, particularly in the recent past, has been fast, vast, varied, diversified and complex. As we have seen in previous chapters, the institutionalisation of distance education in India had its beginning in the establishment of Institutes of Correspondence Courses, some of which were subsequently renamed as Directorates/Institutes of Distance Education in dual mode Universities. Recently, the emergence and establishment of single mode distance education institutions such as Open Universities has heralded a new era in distance education. Due to establishment of distinct units/structures for performing different activities related to distance education and increased division of labour, the organisational structure has become complex. Of course, it has become essential to provide mass(ive) and democratic education to all the needy and deprived sections of the society.

As a sequel to the efforts of open and distance education institutions various and diversified programmes leading to degrees (graduate, post-graduate and research), diplomas (graduate and post-graduate) and certificates have been launched in Arts. Commerce, Science, Engineering and Technology, Computers and other faculties. Besides these, a few non-credit courses/programmes are also on offer. Multi-media publicity to distance education programmes and admission of students through different methods and modes—direct, through entrance test and on-line mode—has multiplied the student enrolment manifold. Accordingly, delivery of the programmes has become diversified. Students are exposed to varied learning experiences such as Self-Instructional Materials, audio, video, radio, and television programmes, teleconferences, assignments, work experiences, seminars, projects, practical, etc. at different places. At the same time they are subjected to diverse methods and techniques of assessment and evaluation.

In order to enhance access and delivery of different programmes to different clientele/ groups of learners, the existing open and distance education institutions have been increasingly collaborating with various conventional, non-conventional, Government and non-Government organisations/agencies in educational and other fields at different levels. Simultaneously new institutions or centres of distance and open education have also been coming into existence. Both full-time and part-time, permanent and temporary personnel have been appointed at different levels for providing diverse services through them to distance learners. In addition, the exploitation of multiple media or multimedia for educational innovations has enhanced the pace of growth of educational technology. All these have contributed to diversification in development and delivery of distance education programmes and particularly in provision of support services to students. These developments together indicate not only the magnitude and pace of development of distance education, but also give the panoramic view of the diverse operations involved in it.

Nevertheless, the increasing pace of development of distance education in all probability can lead to terrifying problems, and difficulties related to development, delivery, management, monitoring and evaluation of distance education programmes. Moreover, in the absence of adequate research base on the effectiveness of different collaborations and innovations, either continuing and expanding such collaborations or forging new ones will be detrimental to the credibility of the system itself. In India, there is not any feasibility study conducted prior to entering into such collaborations. In the absence of such studies, the programmes through new collaborations, should be delivered purely on pilot or experimental basis. During such pilot runs of the programme systematic feedback should be obtained on each kind of collaborative offer of programmes.

There is also a need for action research to be undertaken by all the units of collaborating institutions for identifying the problems, bottlenecks and weaknesses on continuous basis with a view to improving the effectiveness of their activities. Till date there is little feedback and action research done on delivery of distance and open education programmes in India. Even this little work is done in an unsystematic or unscientific manner and not worthy to mention here. Everything related to delivery of programmes through collaborations is being done on trial and error basis in an enterprising and ambitious manner. Another laxity is the absence of an in-built feedback mechanism on every new activity being undertaken to deliver the programmes. All these speak for the need, urgency and magnitude of the feedback and action research on delivery of distance education programmes. Therefore, the institutions and the personnel involved in every new collaborative activity should carry out feedback and action research for identifying and removing the bottlenecks and problems in implementation of the programmes and for improving their efficiency. The feedback studies should be time bound and short duration studies in respect of a few selected activities.

Like in any other field, research and development are the two co-existing and mutually supportive elements in the field of education as well. This should be more so in the case of emerging fields or systems such as distance education, particularly in developing counties like India. Furthering of research at the cost of development or vice-versa would lead, at some point or the other, to such consequences as wastage of resources—human, material and financial. In view of the quantitative expansion of distance education in India, and the weak research base for such expansion one can infer that the research in distance education is not commensurate with its development. This calls for extensive, qualitative and rapid research with emphasis on action and feedback research which can help in preventing or arresting the evil consequences that might arise from unsound and quantitative expansion of the existing system.

It is, thus, clear that the action and feedback research is almost a neglected area in distance education in India. Hence there is an urgency for action and feedback research in distance education. Therefore, this chapter attempts to highlight the priority areas for action and feedback research in distance education. The priority areas identified here will be of paramount use to the potential researchers in choosing topics for focused research and providing sufficient insight into these areas.

Some of the priority areas—broad and key—for action and feedback research in distance education in India are given below:

A. *Publicity Outreach*

Distance education institutions, particularly Open Universities, have been publicising and popularising their programmes through different media, means and ways. But, there is little research done in respect of the effectiveness, extent of outreach, and merits and demerits of these varied publicity efforts. Some of the specific priority areas of research under this area are:

- *(a)* The extent of publicity outreach (overall and specific through particular medium) through radio, television, press and other printed materials, and through face-to-face by personnel directly involved at different levels;
- *(b)* The relative efficiency and cost effectiveness of the publicity efforts through different media, means, methods and techniques in certain geographically disadvantaged areas such as North-Eastern States;

(c) Public and target group perception and receptivity of publicity efforts through different media vis-à-vis different programmes in different geographical areas;

(d) The disadvantages, limitations and weaknesses of different publicity efforts in respect of a particular programme in a particular area and the measures required for increasing the impact of these publicity efforts through different media; and

(e) The extent of suitability of publicity efforts through different media, means and methods to different target groups in different geographical areas.

B. *Identifying, Developing and Launching of Diverse Programmes*

Variety of conventional and non-conventional programmes have been launched and are being launched year after year. But there is no proper context evaluation being done for assessing the actual demand of the target group and identification and launching of suitable programmes for them in selected geographical areas. Nor there is systematic feedback on the programmes even after launching them in those areas. Some of the specific priority sub-areas under this area are:

(a) The context evaluation of the actual demand for developing and launching a particular programme;

(b) Sustainability of a particular programme in terms of the continuity of demand over a reasonable period of time in different localities;

(c) Receptivity of a programme by the target group with a view to re-evaluating the context for suitable modifications in the programme.

C. *Admission/ Enrolment/Registration of Students*

Different procedures have been followed for admitting the students to different programmes, depending upon their nature, duration, etc. This applies to programmes offered by the same institution or by different institutions. Also periodicity of admission of students to different programmes varies depending upon the length or duration of programmes. Admission is done once a year for some programmes, twice a year for some programmes and round the year for some other programmes. Further, only one mode of admission is followed for some programmes, lateral admission for some programmes and even multiple modes of admission for some other programmes. Thus, the extent of openness or flexibility in terms of admission varies from programme to programme. There are restrictions on in-take of students for some programmes while there is no restriction for other programmes. There is need for action and feedback research into all these aspects to identify the problems and flexibilities vis-à-vis different programmes depending on their nature, duration etc. Some of the significant priority sub-areas for such research under this area are:

(a) The advantages, disadvantages and efficiency of admission of students into different programmes only once a year, twice a year, and round the year;

(b) The advantages, disadvantages, efficiency and limitations of admitting students into different programmes through single mode only, through lateral entries and through multiple modes;

(c) Comparative study of the effectiveness of admitting students into different programmes through different ways/modes.

(d) A viable/minimum, optimum and maximum number of students for each of the programmes.

D. Diversified Delivery of Programmes

Depending upon the objectives, target group, nature and duration of programmes the delivery mechanisms have been different for different programmes. Even the same programme can be delivered in different ways or methods. Some distance education institutions deliver their programmes through correspondence mode with a provision for contact sessions/ programmes while some other institutions follow muti-media approach with a provision for student support services through a wide network of Regional Centres, Study Centres, work centres, multi-media learning centres, satellite learning centres and so on at different places. These centres utilise the expertise of different kinds of people for different programmes. There is endless expansion and diversity in delivery mechanism including support services in variety of ways. But, there is little research carried out in this area as well. Given below are some of the priority sub-areas under this area which demand action and feedback research.

(a) The problems in delivery of programmes through a particular media method/mode/mechanism only and through their combination;
(b) Identification of the programmes best suited for delivery through more than one medium/method/mode/mechanism.
(c) Advantages and disadvantages of delivering a programme through different media as alternatives to each other.
(d) Comparative Study of delivery of different programmes through different media, methods and mechanisms.

E. Collaborations with different agencies/organisations: For production and delivery of programmes the distance education institutions or Open Universities have entered and have been entering into different kinds of collaborations, through various memoranda of understanding, agreements, contracts, etc. with various Government, private and voluntary agencies/organisations at national and international level. Different activities have been undertaken by different agencies/organisations with different financial commitments and sharing of manpower, physical and material resources. But there is need for action and feedback research to assess and improve the efficiency of these collaborations. The following can be considered as the priority sub-areas for action and feedback research under this area.

(a) The mutual benefits to and commitments from both distance education institutions or open universities and the collaborating agencies/organisations in respect of a particular programme(s).

(b) A comparative study of advantages and disadvantages of different types of collaborations with different agencies/organisations in respect of a particular programme or different programmes on comparative basis.

(c) Identification of major problems of collaborations vis-à-vis type of agencies/organizations—Govt., Private, Voluntary, etc.

(d) A comparative study of collaborations with institutions/organization at national and international level.

(e) Special problems and advantages of multiple collaborations with an institution at national and/or at international level.

F. *Examinations and Evaluation*

Different programmes of the same institution or same programme of different institutions have/has different evaluation systems and procedures with variations in continuous and terminal evaluations. Periodicity and flexibility in conduct of examinations also vary from programme to programme and from institution to institution. Adequate action and feedback research on examinations and evaluation of different programmes of an institution or of a particular programme of different institutions would help in strengthening the evaluation system and in improving the standards. Some of the important sub-areas that require action and feedback research under this area are as follows:

(a) A comparative study of the strengths and weaknesses of the same type of examinations and evaluation systems being followed by one particular institution in respect of its different programmes and by different distance education institutions or universities in respect of a particular programme.

(*b*) Common problems of different distance education institutions or universities in respect of examinations and evaluation of students of different programmes with and without practical components.

The broad areas and priority sub-areas of action and feedback research which are identified, as above, are not complete and exhaustive. Nevertheless, these areas help in identifying many more broad and key priority areas for conduct of action and feedback research. These would also help in taking timely and appropriate measures for improving the efficiency of the personnel involved and for effective implementation of different activities related to different programmes through different collaborations and delivery mechanisms.

Section - III

Maximising the Reach

8

The Future of Distance Education and Distance Education of the Future

Since distance education is essentially based on technology, its development at global and national level has been greatly influenced by advancement in information and communication technology (ICT). But, the exploitation of ICT for distance education has not been uniform across the globe. This has been due to availability, access and affordability differential by different countries. Accordingly, the growth and development of distance education in different countries and continents varied significantly.

There are many under developed countries which are struggling hard to enhance access to simpler technology like audio, video cassettes, radio and good quality print. The developed countries, that fall on the other extreme, have both access and affordability to the most advanced and highly interactive technologies of the day. The developing countries falling in between, suffer from either non-availability of technology, or lack of access to it or inability to afford it. As a result, the share of developed, developing and underdeveloped countries in ICT is quite unequal. This can be substantiated by citing a study by Suriya (1998, pp. 161-67). He (Suriya) studied the ICT status of 50 sample countries by taking into account the print media, accessibility, radio penetration, television penetration, telephone density, mobile phone density, fax machine density, number of internet hosts, and computer density. He found that the high income nations possessed more than 55 percent of the global ICT infrastructure, while the upper and the lower middle income nations held about 36 percent and the low income nations about 9 percent.

In such a situation, the future of distance education in terms of its prospects and functions would be bright, but the level and quality of ICT used would vary very widely in different countries. Nevertheless, distance education in future is not going to be equally promising for all the countries and for all the people (sections) in a country. Therefore, ICT strategy would rather work as an effective strategy to promote equality among the equals while perpetuating or even widening inequality among the unequal. The basic objectives of this chapter, therefore, are to present the :

(i) future of distance education with a view to highlighting its prospects; and
(ii) distance education of the future that could work as a strategic tool to perpetuate inequality among the un-equals in the global context.

Let me first touch upon the future of distance education.

The Future of Distance Education

Distance Education has been evolving along with advancement in information and communication technology. Taylor's (1996) description of evolution of distance education at University of Southern Queensland (USQ) in Toowoomba, Australia appears to have universal significance. The framework developed by him outlines four generations of distance education delivery technologies and identifies each generation with a model. These generations and models can be summed up as follows:

1. First generation with *correspondence model* utilizing print media;
2. Second generation with *multimedia model* utilizing print, audio-tape, computer based learning (CML/ CAL), Interactive video (disc and tape);
3. Third generation with *tele-learning model* utilizing audio and video conferencing, audio-graphic communication, broadcast, TV/Radio plus audio-teleconferencing; and
4. Fourth generation with *flexible learning model* utilizing interactive multimedia (IMM), internet based access to WWW resources and computer mediated communication.

One can clearly observe that there is increase in the degree or level of sophistication and interactivity of the technology used from generation to generation or from model to model. As Cronk and Mclendon (1999) rightly observed the delivery generations of distance education are not mutually exclusive and discrete. Some providers of distance education programmes may be operating across more than one generation or model at a time. For instance, even if the number of programmes characterized by fourth generation is more at any time the programmes operating across the first three generations may also continue to account for good proportion of clientele of a distance education provider. This may be true with respect to different providers in different countries in the world in general and among the underdeveloped and developing countries in particular .

The future of distance education depends primarily on the development and creative use of new technologies by adhering to the relevant regulations. The telecommunications tools lead the way in newer technology (Porter, 1997,p.16). Today the knowledge media which arise from the convergence of computing, telecommunications and the cognitive sciences are brining new possibilities to improve teaching and learning systems of open universities. This gives a perspective of the virtual universities and the knowledge media would help in reinforcing the quality by way of providing better course material, student support services, logistics and research (Daniel, 1996 and 1997).

Distance education would be able to provide learning opportunities to people any where in the world. The technology is enabling its reach to any place to any number of people at any time, and usually for a reasonable cost. It can provide materials to them in a single medium, two media or multiple media and in different formats to meet different learners' preferences in accordance with their learning styles, needs and abilities. It can bring people together to discuss ideas and share information, and it will have the potential for being a highly efficient, effective and innovative form of education and training. In such a situation, there will be different kinds of virtual classrooms all over the world. According to Porter (1997, pp.23-40) creation of virtual classroom becomes possible through a mix of technological tools and methods such as surface mail correspondence, broadcast, audio-tape, videotape,, telecast, e-mail correspondence, web site, cable television or closed circuit television, teleconferencing, desktop videoconferencing and so on.

By looking at the global perspective and prospects of emerging technologies, media mix, knowledge media and models of delivery discussed above the future of distance education can be generally visualized as follows:

1. In all countries where distance education is yet to gain ground, the course of distance education development would pass through certain generations of its delivery over a period of time. In general, in an underdeveloped country with little access to advanced technology it will be generation-1 to generation-2 to generation-3 to generation-4. As far as institutions are concerned mostly there will be a beginning in the form of dual mode institutions, followed by emergence of single mode distance and open education institutions and then consortia of

single and dual mode distance and open education institutions.

2. Technological revolution resulting from enhanced access and affordability to technology will increase the pace and quality of distance education. Technology helps in bringing revolutionary changes in all the activities—course development, admission of students, course delivery, student evaluation and certification. It would be possible to have multiple points of entry, online admissions, online delivery of courses, online evaluation, on demand examinations, online certification, and so on.
3. There will be acceleration in the process of globalization of distance education. Its rapid expansion, quàntitative and qualitative, will be the order of its future. It enhances the pace of achievement of learñing, progressive and knowledge society.
4. Adoption of advanced interactive delivery technologies such as computer mediated learning (CML) or computer aided learning (CAL), CD-ROM internet hybrid, course-on-line (COL), web-based instruction, e-mail, etc. will increase at alarming rate. Sharing of information and interaction between teachers and learners take place at a common denominator, but at altogether a different and higher plane i.e. in virtual campus mode. Also, as a sequel to asynchronous delivery of curriculum, extensive and intensive interaction, and frequent up-gradation of curriculum the distance teaching-learning process becomes not only more and more dynamic but also a subject of intensive and extensive public auditing. The isolation between and among the distance teachers and learners is reduced drastically, and thus, the didactic process would become more dynamic. However, the changing nature, character and scope of the processes of course preparation, development, delivery, assessment and evaluation

would enhance the objectivity, flexibility and overall quality of distance education.

5. The increasing scope for virtual learning environments or virtual classrooms paves ways for formation of virtual campuses or universities in all countries and global university(ies) at global level.
6. The increase in collaborative, networked and interactive teaching-learning models provides to the learners a wide choice to choose from diverse, efficient, fast and cost-effective means of education. Also, increasing collaboration between distance and open education institutions, business organizations and industry will promote effective and efficient pooling and sharing of resources to realize the common objectives of the collaborating institutions.
7. Different countries will witness rapid growth of professional associations of distance and open education and their networking at national and international level. As a result, the process of global sharing of information, experience, resources, expertise, etc. would strengthen a lot.
8. Rapid expansion and increasing acceptability of distance and open education will lead to convergence of conventional, dual mode and single mode distance and open education institutions within a country and across the countries. Consequently, there will be an increase in the transfer of credits of students between and among different courses and programmes of all these institutions at national and international level.
9. The future roles and responsibilities of distance teacher and learner, the nature and character of curriculum, its design, development and delivery will change and the tangible structures of the open and distance education universities and institutions might disappear gradually. These changes become significant particularly with emergence of virtual campuses, global universities or online universities and the like.

10. Distance and open education institutions, through effective and judicious use of technologies, will acquire all potentials to pave the way for educational explosion in different countries. Thus, educational explosion would help in addressing the educational challenges posed by population explosion, knowledge explosion and information explosion. Samara (1999, pp 1-2) says: "one of the most effective ways of conveying information to huge sections of populations is through open learning. Though the potential of open learning, in the context of distance education, is enormous it would become a reality in the very near future through the digital transmission, in addition to the audio broadcast facilitated by the constellation of geo-stationery satellites to be launched by the World Space Organization."

Distance Education of the Future

Distance and open education is considered to be an effective instrument to democratize education, to enhance access to education, to provide equal opportunity, and to impart quality education for all. In fact, this is true to some extent only. The reality is and would be that distance education of the future will work more as a strategy to perpetuate and/or to widen the existing inequalities rather than to promote equality between and among different individuals, institutions, countries and the continents. This is because of the fact that the distance education of the future is not going to be equally promising for all the continents, countries, institutions, sections of population and the individuals. It means, it helps in promotion of equality among only those who enjoy equal economic, educational and technological status, while it perpetuates or enhances the inequality among the non-equals.

In the global sense, distance education in the future would create generation gaps between and among different countries across the globe and also different institutions within a country. While majority of the underdeveloped countries will be toiling with first generation distance education, developed countries will continue to go ahead with new generations and beyond the existing models of distance education. Perhaps, the developing countries will remain in between. In addition to this, the inequalities between and within different regions, continents and countries vis-à-vis distance education generations/models would continue to widen.

There has been north-south inequalities in distance and open education on the globe in general. One can clearly notice inequalities between and among the continents within the North—North America, Europe and Asia or within the South—South America, Africa and Australia by_taking the entire continent as a unit for comparision. As far as the inequalities within a continent are concerned, Aguti's (1996) study on African Virtual University (AVU), which was established for the Sub-Sahara African countries, can be cited as the most appropriate example. This is so because it *(AVU) has created distance education generation gap between the group of countries that joined it and the other group which did not join it.*

If we believe that knowledge is power and technology is a tool or means for information and knowledge, then there is every possibility of the globe getting divided into there groups of countries. First, consisting of advanced and powerful countries that have enough access to rich information and technology, second, underdeveloped countries having poor access to information and technology, and third, developing countries having moderate access to information and technology. In other words, there will be a group of elite countries which have quick, less costly and effective access to information while there will be a group of countries which are marginalized in terms of access and affordability to both technology and information. Of course, in between there will be a group of countries having moderate access to technology and information with moderate affordability. Thus, the gap between the information and technology haves and have-nots increases drastically.

The virtual, global universities will succeed in globalising quality education through the use of hyper media and through the delivery of global information resources at the doors of richer learners than others. Further, the cross cultural differences in sharing and utilizing the global information and resources will give an edge to the learners from advanced cultures compared to their counterparts from other cultures. This gives rise to a situation where the individual learners from the advanced cultures advance at a faster rate than those from other cultures. Also, at the providers level, there will be two groups—one, advanced providers as leaders and, the other, as follower-promoters of the former's agenda. Because of the use of hyper-tech the curriculum would be highly dynamic and its transaction becomes both synchronous and asynchronous. Evaluation activities take place at a higher plane. Though this helps in democratizing and enhancing equal opportunities for quick, cheap and quality education there is every likelihood of such education system suffering from the dangers of proxy students working for distance learners if adequate checks are not put. As Jenkins (1998, p. 118) points out, in distance education we are accustomed to trust our learners through reliance on self-assessment and assignments completed unsupervised. The growing ubiquity of networked learning gives new importance to trust. Policing activity on the internet is virtually impossible. No passwords or protective tools can prevent abuse of trust by a student who is determined to cheat. Inevitably, this will happen from time to time. Such behaviour can be confronted by encouraging the development of a culture of individual responsibility for learning.

Moreover, the culture and process of research in open and distance education are different from those of traditional one. Now research reports—even preliminary findings—can be posted on the internet. Such openness and access encourage the rapid spread of new knowledge on one hand but raises questions as well about safety and security of the intellectual property on the other. Where do we draw the line between sharing knowledge and unauthorized use of ideas which belong to another? (Jenkins, 1998). Frequently changing laws related to copy rights, patents, and trademarks and the issues surrounding them have incited heated debates, nationally and internationally. In addition, tracking down persons who infringe on the fair use of protected information across national borders may be more than frustrating; it may be next to impossible, unless the misuse of the originator's expression of an idea or a concept is brought to his or her attention (Porter, 1997, p. 207). Given this kind of distance education of the future, the kind of issues, problems and challenges it poses and dangers it brings to the intellectual community of the world are too serious and complex to be solved.

Conclusion

The future of distance education in terms of its role and prospects will be bright and it would be able to acquire all the potential to address the diverse and ever changing educational needs and challenges of the global society. While knowledge and information explosion coupled with technological revolution could help distance education trigger educational explosion, its effects and consequences the world over would vary widely. The issues of copyright, intellectual property rights and fair use of information by both distance education providers and clientele, amongst others, are to be addressed adequately in the environment of global competition, networking and resource sharing. Then only the distance education of the future will be equally promising and highly democratizing force for all.

References

Aguti, N.J. (1999). "One Year of Virtual University Experience at Makerere University in Uganda", *Proceedings of PAN Commonwealth Forum on Open Learning: Empowerment through knowledge and technology*, held at Bander Seri Begawan, Brunei Darussalam from 1-5 March, 1999.

Cronk, P., and Mclendon, E. (1999). "Issues in the Management of Online Tertiary Education Programmes in Australia". *Proceedings of PAN Commonwealth Forum* op.cit.

Daniel, John, S. (1996). *Mega-Universities and Knowledge Media: Technology Strategies for Higher Education,* London: Kogan Page.

Daniel, John, S. (1997). "Mega-Universities, Virtual Universities and Knowledge Media: Can We Have Quantity with Quality?". *Keynote Address at the 11th Annual Conference of Asian Association of Open Universities on Quality Assurance in Distance and Open Learning* held at Kuala Lumpur, Malaysia from 11-14 November, 1997.

Jenkins, J. (1998). "Distance Education, The Internet and Learning Culture (Behavioural and Cultural Issues involved in networked and collaborative learning)". Paper presented at the *International Conference on Collaborative Networked Learning,* held at the Indira Gandhi National Open University, New Delhi from 16-18 February, 1998.

Porter, L.R. (1997). Creating the Virtual Classroom: *Distance Learning with the Internet.* New York: John Wiley and Sons, Inc.

Samara, N. (1999). "Affordable Technology for People in Developing Countries", *Keynote Address at PAN Commonwealth Forum on Open Learning,* op.cit.

Suriya, M. (1998), "Technological Strategies for Collaborative Learning and Partnership Programmes among the Developed and Developing Countries", *International Conference on Collaborative Networked Learning,* op.cit.

Taylor, J.C. (1996). "Perspectives on the Educational Uses of Technology", *Report of the International Council of Distance Education Standing Conference of Presidents*: Task Force on Educational Technologies, Norway: Lillehammer.

9

The Unreached Distance Learners: A Typological Perspective

When the communication and information technology is developing fast the globe is shrinking faster into a small global village. As has been presented in chapter-8, the information and communication technology has been changing the future of distance education. Today majority of the people and places have access to some technology or the other, in some form or the other. In this context, the immense potential of (distance)education technology to reach any place, to any number of people at any time cannot be undermined. In such a state-of-the-art situation of distance education (technology) it would be painful to hear of the people and places educationally unreached yet. At the same time, how they are unreached cannot be ignored. There may be many unreached in many senses, but they need to be defined and identified properly. Then and only then it would be possible to reach them effectively and adequately. It is precisely what has been attempted in this chapter from the typological perspective.

In India, ever since the institutionalization of distance education started in 1962 with establishment of School of Correspondence Courses in University of Delhi at Delhi, it (distance education) has been progressing in leaps and bounds. According to IGNOU (2000a) there are 62 Institutes of

Correspondence Courses/Directorates of Distance Education and 10 Open Universities (1 National Open University and 9 State Open Universities) offering distance education courses/ programmes at higher education level. In addition to these, there are many other professional bodies and institutes offering specialized professional, technical and vocational programmes. Thus, at present, the distance education system at tertiary level can be said to consist of more than 72 distance and open education institutes/universities with more than 50 regional centers, 3000 study, programme and other kind of centers and a large number of partner institutions located in different parts of the country. There is a National Open School (NOS) with some State Open Schools established in some States which cater to school dropouts and children who cannot attend formal schools for pursuing secondary and senior secondary education. At this level i.e. secondary and senior secondary level, there were 6 Regional Centres, 667 Study Centres/ Accredited Institutions and 144 Accredited Vocational Institutes in the country in 1998 (National Open School, 1998) while the same have increased to 7, 730 and 206 respectively in 1999 (NOS, 1999) under NOS alone.

A word on the magnitude and rate of growth of the programmes. At higher/tertiary education level, there were 104 programmes with 841 courses on offer by just four Open Universities in 1995 (Distance Education Council, 1995), but the number of programmes and courses now on offer by IGNOU alone were 47 and 553 respectively in 1999 (IGNOU, 1999) and 50 and 604 respectively in 2000 (IGNOU, 2000b). These programmes and courses have been catering to the needs and interests of students with diverse socio-economic and demographic profile—general and reserved categories, formal and non-formal streams, males and females, rural and urban, employed and unemployed, married and unmarried, disadvantaged and disabled, and so on.

The programmes on offer at tertiary level include a wide variety of general programmes covering the faculties of Arts, Commerce and Sciences, besides various professional, technical and vocational programmes in education, distance education, medicine, nursing, journalism and mass communication, business management, computer and information science, tourism, library and information science, public relations, agriculture, sericulture, gardening, electronics, hotel management and so on. There are wide ranging courses on offer at secondary and senior secondary level as well covering different academic subjects which are very flexibly combined with many vocational subjects in the areas of house wiring, electrical appliances repairing, motor and transformer rewinding, radio and tape recorder repairing, television repairing, cutting and tailoring, dress making, refrigeration and air conditioning, typewriting, word processing, jute production technology, carpentry, solar energy technician, bio-gas energy technician, bakery and confectionery, laundry services, stenography, secretarial practice, plant protection, water management for crop production, mushroom production technology, furniture and cabinet making, electroplating, house keeping, catering management, food processing, play center management and so on. These programmes at different levels lead to certificate, diploma, degree (graduate), post-graduate degrees and even Ph.D. The programmes are thus of diverse nature and type such as educational, vocational, professional, training and awareness available in the medium of English and many recognized Indian languages. Yet, there may be people and places unreached in different terms through distance and open learning.

Need for Defining "The Unreached"

Notwithstanding the above, and despite the tremendous potential of distance education to reach any person, anywhere and any time, the reach of distance education, particularly hundred per cent reach in all respects, cannot be taken as granted for. Therefore, defining and identifying the unreached through Distance and Open Learning assumes greater significance in enhancing not only the reach but also the efficiency of distance and open education. In this context, there is a need to define the term "unreached" in possible detail. Though the term appears to be very simple to understand, it is difficult to define in the context of distance and open education/learning. At the out set, it is essential to establish clearly all the possible contexts in which "the unreached" can be posited. We, therefore, need to make clear to ourselves the terms in which we define the term 'unreached'. Is it in terms of: the potential learners/target groups of the particular programes(s) who are unreached? or the social groups, sections, classes, etc. hitherto unreached? or the geographical areas not covered so far in whatever the manner? or the learners on roll to whom the programmes have not been delivered effectively? or is it in terms of all the above? or in any other terms? All these need to be dovetailed. Furthermore, does it not include those individuals, groups and places that could not have access to the existing programmes and those for whom there are no relevant programmes on offer by the distance and open education institutes? It, therefore, requires a comprehensive look at defining the term "unreached" vis-à-vis different types of unreached through distance and open learning.

A Typological Perspective

From the foregoing paragraph we can understand that defining the term "unreached" through distance and open learning in precise terms would be very difficult task. But, at the same time it is imperative to define it in concrete terms in order to facilitate any meaningful efforts to reach them.

In order to define the term "unreached" from typological perspective it is essential to identify different and possible types of unreached. The unreached can be broadly classified as follows:

- *(i)* Geographically unreached
- *(ii)* Technologically unreached
- *(iii)* Unreached among the target groups
- *(iv)* Unrached among the disadvantaged
- *(v)* Unreached among the "so called reached"

Though the unreached have been conveniently divided under the above broad types they cannot be treated as either exhaustive and exclusive types nor can they be treated as water-tight compartment like hard and fast types.

(i) Geographically unreached

The geographically unreached through distance and open learning can be further conceived in various ways. To list a few, they can be as follows:

(a) States/Union Territories in India which do not have an established

- single mode distance and Open University (e.g. there are 16 States without the Open University of their own)
- dual mode institute (i.e. conventional institute with an ICC/DDE) (e.g. there are 7 States without an ICC/DDE established in any University located in those States.
- single or dual mode open and distance education institute
- regional centre of national open university.

(b) Districts which do not have an established

- regional centre of national open university
- regional centre of a state open university
- regional centre of national or a state open university
- study centre of either national or state open university

(c) Other Areas which do not have any centre of any distance and open education institute.

(ii) Technologically unreached

Ranga Rao (1999) emphasises the relevance, potential and effectiveness of electronic media and teleconference in distance education, particularly in reaching the unreached among the enrolled students of Dr. B.R. Ambedkar Open University, Andhra Pradesh who are unable to utilise the audio, video materials and teleconference facility at study centres for various reasons. While thorough reaching of all those on rolls is very important, reaching those who are not on rolls of any institute/university is much more important. In this context, it is all the more important to identify the technologically unreached. These can be those individuals, groups of individuals or the places/areas that could not be reached through any one medium or through combination of selected media or all the media together which are used for offering distance and open education programmes. On this basis, for instance, the technologically unreached can again be conveniently identified as the following sub-types:

(a) Unreached through print materials
(b) Unreched through Radio
(c) Unreached through TV
(d) Unreached through teleconference, videoconference, etc.
(e) Unreached through e-mail, fax and other electronic or online mode
(f) Unreached through particular combination of media
(g) Unreached through multimedia package as a whole.

Here it is even important to identify the regional, study and other kind of centres where the programmes are on offer and do not have access to any one or two or more or all the above technologies, amongst others.

Also, it can include the programmes which are not available in any one or different media as self contained alternative self-instructional materials.

(iii) Unrached among the target groups

Under this type will fall all those potential learners in the relevant age group who could not get admitted into the courses/programmes of either the formal institutions or of the open and distance education institutions. To put it more succinctly these learners would fall in or become a part of one or more or all the above broad types of the unreached. These can be conveniently and generally sub-grouped under the following:

(a) gender-wise unreached — unreached males and females
(b) place or area-wise unreached —the unreached rural, urban and tribals
(c) the employed unreached — the general, technical, professional and other category of staff or those in the unorganized sectors of employment.
(d) unemployed unreached — the illiterate, literate, unskilled, skilled and the academically well qualified unemployed
(e) any other special groups such as prisoners, ex-prisoners, old aged, and the like.

If one looks at these target groups from the points of view of the nature, level, medium and other aspects of the programme they can be divided as follows:

(a) *Unreached through unreaching content*
This type of learners are those who are unable to learn anything or many things from the materials or unable to cope up with the difficulty level and style of language, level and load of the subject content and the like. The identification of sub-types of unreached under this type is very difficult as the processes to be followed for the purpose will be very difficult and studious. Yet, identification of this kind of unreached would help a lot in revising the courses and even the entire programme.

(b) *Unreached due to non-availability of relevant programmes*
This type includes those of target group or population for whom there are no specific and relevant programmes developed by distance and open education institutes. This type is very comprehensive and includes or covers large chunk of the unreached.

(c) *Linguistically unreached*

These are those for whom there is neither a programme specially developed in their own language/mother tongue nor the existing programmes are offered in their language or mother tongue. The unreaching style and level of language in presenting the content to the learners also add to the linguistically unreached. Here, identification of programmes and their media of instruction is essential to translate them into other languages in which they can be offered.

(iv) Unreached among the disadvantaged

These can be those for whom there are programmes/courses on offer, but are unable to take advantage of the same because of the disadvantages they suffer from. The unreached among the disadvantaged can be considered as follows:

(a) Unreached among the economically or financially disadvantaged groups/sections who could not afford to pay the programme fees and/or bear the distance education programme cost.

(b) Unreached among the socially backward castes and classes who are unable to cope up with the distance mode of teaching and learning.

(c) Unreached among the physically disabled.

The unreached among the physically disabled can be further divided into the following types from the view point of the specific disability(ies) they suffer from.

(a) the unreached among the orthopadically disabled
(b) The unreached among the mentally disabled
(c) The unreached among the blind
(d) The unreached among the visually impaired
(e) The unreached among the deaf
(f) The unreached among the hearing impaired
(g) The unreached among the dumb
(h) The unreached among the voice impaired

Distance education has got tremendous potential to reach any or all categories of the disadvantaged, yet the disabled remain the most challenging among them. This is more so when the disabled suffer from multiple disabilities.

(v) Unreached among the "so called reached"

This type includes all those students who have been enrolled, admitted, or registered in various courses or programmes but either dropped out subsequently or failed to complete their courses or programmes. The magnitude of drop outs and inactive students or non-performers constitute the unreached among the "so called reached". When the institute fails massively to deliver the programme to the enrolled students due to any reason their plight becomes worse than that of any other unreached groups.

Conclusion

From the above typology of the unreached it is clear that the unreached can be of different types and sub-types. One can understand that there could be other approaches to defining the unreached through distance and open education/learning. However, based on the typology of the unreached discussed above, the author would like to offer a comprehensive definition of "the unreached" in the following terms.

The unreached through the distance and open education/ learning can be defined as those individuals or groups, classes or sections of individuals in any geographical area who could not be reached due to:

- *(a)* non-existence of specific or relevant programme(s) on offer in their mother tongue or desired medium of instruction suitable to them;
- *(b)* ineffective, defective, inadequate delivery of the existing programmes to them; and/or
- *(c)* the content of the programme presented in one technological medium or media mix or multiple media is not compatible with their level and abilities.

While offering this definition the considerations such as viability of a programme, problem of resources, cost-effectiveness etc., of either the existing programmes or the programmes needed or to be developed to reach the unreached have not been taken into account. It is hoped that this definition would help the distance and open education institutions in identifying more and more types of the unreached in precise terms and also in coming up with appropriate programmes and strategies relevant to different individuals, groups and sections in different areas/places hitherto unreached on one hand and to revise the courses and programmes on offer for their effective delivery on the other.

References

Distance Education Council (1995). "*Open Universities in India: Academic Programmes—1995*", New Delhi: Indira Gandhi National Open University.

IGNOU (1999). *Indira Gandhi National Open University: A Profile—1999*, New Delhi: IGNOU.

IGNOU (2000a). *Distance Education Council*, New Delhi: IGNOU.

IGNOU (2000b). *IGNOU Profile 2000*. New Delhi: IGNOU.

National Open School (1998). *National Open School: Annual Report—1997-98*. New Delhi: National Open University (Unpublished).

National Open School (1999). *Prospectus—1999-2000*, New Delhi: National Open School.

Ranga Rao, C.V. (1999). "Reaching the Unreached: Experience of an Open University", *University News*, Vol. 37, No. 42, October 18.

10

Towards a Consortium for Distance Education in India: Issues and Problems

Need for Distance Education Consortium

Distance education in India has, as at present, developed into a system almost parallel to that of conventional education. Of course, both the systems have merged with each other at different levels and in different areas of activities of distance education. Notwithstanding this, there have been efforts to offer non-conventional and conventional programmes and courses by distance education institutes/universities. While it has not ended there, some of the subsequently established distance and open education institutes/universities have been duplicating these distance education programmes and courses, and some others have adopted these courses/programmes. Since distance education is basically dependant on delivery of different kinds of materials developed in different media, offering similar programmes and courses by different institutes involves a lot of wastage in the form of duplication of efforts in establishing delivery system and mechanisms. Thus, there is duplication of efforts not only in developing the course materials but also in establishing the student support system for delivery of these programmes. In doing so, the differences are bound to arise in quality of the materials, the delivery of support services and the programmes as a whole offered by these institutes/universities. Further, if the curriculum of a programme offered by these institutions/universities varies widely, it will reduce the opportunities for inter-institutional transfer of students because of problems related credit transfer. This will be a hindrance for pursuance of their education as per their (changing) needs, problems, demands, interests, etc. caused by their mobility of different kinds.

Distance education will be more meaningful if it is made more accessible, relevant, flexible and open. To enhance students' access to various courses and programmes of different institutes and universities there must be multiple points or outlets which are equally and easily accessible to different categories of needy students. In order to make distance education relevant the programmes must be tailored to the needs, problems, interests and demands of the learners. To make it more flexible there is a need for introducing relaxations in methods and procedures that allow the students to adjust, to adopt and to cope with needs, demands and problems at different stages of pursuance of their programmes and courses. These flexibilities or relaxations should facilitate or pave way for intra-programme, inter-programme and inter-institutional credit transfer. This should happen without affecting the pace of progress of learner at any cost. Once this becomes possible there is large scope for sustaining the interest and motivation of learners, for reducing their dropout rate and for promoting their pass out rate as well. The enhanced access, relevance, flexibility and openness of the distance education programmes should enable the learner to get entry into any particular programme on offer by any one of these institutions from any access point, to pursue his/her education by being on the rolls of any one of these institutions, and to acquire the appropriate certificates, diplomas or degrees from any one of these institutions. This requires purposive, concerted and well-coordinated efforts facilitated through a consortium of distance and open education institutes/universities in the country. If the conventional institutes/universities can also be involved in the consortium that would help a lot in promoting the parity, quality and standards of education offered through any one or different modes and institutions. Above all, it would enhance the reach of distance and open education to many types of unreached learners discussed in chapter 9.

Relevance of Consortium for Distance Education

Development of a consortium for distance education in India is not an easy task. The distance learners are characterized by different socioeconomic, cultural, linguistic and educational background. The size and geographical, topographic, and climatic variations of the country are also no less. Added to this, the syllabus of a programme, the content and quality of its materials differ from institution to institution. This is further complicated by differences in procedures of admission, assessment, evaluation, etc. of students of these institutions. If the students are to be benefited more from these institutions there is a need for coordination of the programmes of these institutions at all the stages. The consortium of distance education is a possible solution to provide better and more flexible education to distance learners, to promote the interests of distance education institutions and to address quality issues through standardized learning packages, support services, evaluation, etc. At the same time the idea of consortium in India raises many issues and poses various problems to the distance educators, researchers and the policy makers. Identification of these issues and problems would pave a long way in effective planning, organisation, establishment and development of a consortium for distance education.

This chapter is, therefore, devoted to identifying different issues and problems related to development of a consortium for distance education in India. This would help to provide the students with more flexible, open and efficient education on one hand and, to facilitate effective pooling and sharing of courses, programmes, other resources, etc., of different distance education institutes and universities on the other. Further, if these issues and problems are addressed effectively, it (the consortium) would benefit these institutes/ universities and their students a lot.

Consortium for Distance Education—What? And Why?

Prior to attempting at identifying the issues and problems involved in developing a consortium for distance education in India it would be appropriate to understand what a consortium is, and what it is in the context of distance education.

According to Webster (1985, p. 217) consortium is "an association or union; a combination of financial institutions and capitalists for the purpose of carrying into effect some financial operations requiring large sources of capital". This definition conceives consortium in a narrow sense and limits its purpose to financial operations of financial institutions and capitalists only. Three essential elements in this definition are:

- Association, union or combination
- Financial institutions and capitalists
- Financial operation.

Consortium is an international business or a banking agreement or a combination of these for carrying out some operation, especially one requiring extensive financial backing (Longman, 1985, p. 312). This definition confines consortium to only international business combination or agreement for carrying out some operation that requires large financial resources. Two elements that characterize this definition are:

- International agreement
- Operation requiring extensive financial backing.

Hornby (1989, p. 250) defines consortium as a "temporary association of a number of countries, companies, banks, etc., for a common purpose". Two characteristics that are basic to this definition are:

- Temporary association
- Common purpose

This definition appears to be general, relatively broader and related to the association of any kind of organizations in a country or more countries. It is clear that none of the above definitions is comprehensive. In view of this I would like to offer the following definition of consortium which I feel is more broader and may be acceptable to many.

Consortium is a temporary or relatively permanent association or union of institutions or organizations—financial or otherwise, national or international, in a country or in more than one country—formed for a common purpose and involves or requires large capital or finance or other resources. This general definition of consortium needs to be further related to education and then to distance education.

In U.K., consortium, in the context of education, is used as a collective term for peripatetic teachers with specialist skills. In U.S., it is used for a group of schools (usually post-secondary) or libraries that combine selected program(me)s or resources (Terry Page, et.al. 1979, p. 83). It means in U.K. it refers to teachers employed at two or more schools and traveling between them regularly, while in U.S. it refers to the institutions that pool their selected programmes or resources. In other words, in U.K. educational consortium refers to a collection of individual teachers employed in more than one school while in U.S. it denotes a group of selected institutions such as schools or libraries.

The above definitions of consortium in general and in the context of education in particular offer some base for conceiving and defining consortium in the context of distance education.

In the context of distance education a consortium can be defined as a temporary or permanent association of distance education institutes/universities for the common purpose of:

(i) providing easily accessible, relevant, flexible, open and effective education to all the needy, deprived and interested people willing to pursue or continue their education through distance mode of learning; and

(ii) promoting growth and development of distance education institutions and the system as a whole.

Within the purview of this definition of consortium for distance education there is a need to spell out basic or specific purposes of the consortium.

Purposes of Consortium for Distance Education

The basic or specific purposes of the consortium can be:

(i) to establish effective functional linkage between and among different distance education institutions;

(ii) to promote better cooperation, collaboration and coordination between and among member institutions of consortium in respect of development, sharing and maintenance of quality materials (self-instructional materials in print, audio and visual media) of distance education programmes;

(iii) to increase the efficiency of delivery of programmes to learners irrespective of their geographical mobility across the regions and their transfer across programmes and institutions through comprehensive system of support services, evaluation, certification and accreditation; and

(iv) to expand and develop open learning systems along with the member institutions/universities of the consortium.

Prior to focusing on the issues and problems related to consortium for distance education, it would be more appropriate to have a brief look at the status of developments on this front.

Status of Developments

Eighth Five Year Plan 1992-97 (GOI, 1992, p.291) envisages that the National Open School (NOS) is expected to provide programme and resource support to state level open schools. The setting up of National Consortium on Open Education to facilitate accreditation of courses and maintenance of quality through a process of networking and evaluation should be pursued by NOS in cooperation with the Indira Gandhi National Open University (IGNOU). NOS appears to have met this expectation.

A latest folder entitled "NOS: The School that made the Difference" published by National Open School makes it clear that there is the National Consortium for Open Schooling (NCOS) launched in September, 1997 and established under NOS. The basic purpose of NCOS is to facilitate better cooperation, collaboration and expansion of open schooling activities in the learning system. This is the status of efforts made as far as a national consortium for open schooling is concerned.

There have been efforts to set up a national consortium for open higher education through Open Universities. According to Pillai and Naidu (1997, p.99) the Distance Education Council (DEC) has endeavoured to establish a network of open universities (OPENET) in the country. This network has a common pool of programmes, with contributions from all existing open universities, which can then be drawn upon by all the members of the network. These developments, no doubt, open up new possibilities, and offer several strategic options, all of which will have a significant impact on the growth of the distance education system, and its efficiency and cost structure.

It is clear that, the efforts appear to be at rudimentary stage. But, unless, this OPENET is further enlarged to include or cover all Institutes/Directorates of Correspondence Courses/Distance Education in conventional universities along with all other institutions offering education through distance mode it would not be a fully nit one. If the NET covers all the institutions offering higher education through distance mode then it would become a consortium for distance education as far as higher education is concerned. While the functioning of NCOS under NOS needs to be studied for its betterment the OPENET is to be strengthened further by pooling and sharing resources and facilities available for student support and delivery of the programmes as a whole. However, the conceptual and operational framework of OPENET also requires enlargement and a thorough study for its development as a comprehensive consortium for distance education in India.

All the above developments related to consortia in distance education in India, even raise certain issues regarding the nature, type, levels, size, etc., of consortium along with relevant problems. The important issues and problems concerning the consortium are discussed below.

Issues

The conception and organisation of Consortium for Distance Education in India is not an easy task. Moreover, multilingual nature of courses and programmes and their instructional materials with multiple quality compound the practical problems involved in forming effective consortium. Given the diversity of programmes, courses, learners, delivery and evaluation mechanisms and procedures the issues that confront the conception of consortium are many. Given below are the important issues that have relevance to the consortium for distance education in India.

1. What should be the nature and kind of consortium?

   (a) Whether temporary or permanent?
   (b) Whether statutory or non-statutory?
   (c) Whether a national consortium or state consortia?
   (d) Whether all the above kinds of consortia?

2. What are all the levels/stages of education for which consortium is to be conceived?

- School level (upto 10th standard when diversification does not start)
- Intermediate level (only+2 stage)
- Higher education level (degree/graduation and above)

3. Whether there should be only one consortium for each level/stage of education for the entire country or more than one consortium i.e. one for each state?
4. If more than one consortium are required at each level/stage, should there be separate consortium for each of the following type of institution?

   - Single mode distance and open education institutes only
   - Dual mode distance and open education institutes only
   - Specialized institutes offering specialized programmes only
   - All the distance and open education institutes/universities in each State.

5. Whether there is a need for programme-based consortium? If yes,

   (a) Whether a separate consortium is required for:

   - all traditional courses/programmes? or
   - all non-traditional courses/programmes? or
   - all certificate programmes?or
   - all diploma programmes? or
   - all degree/graduate programmes? or
   - all post graduate/master degree programmes? or
   - a combination of programmes and courses?

   (b) Whether a separate consortium is required for

   - all programmes in a selected discipline or a group of disciplines across different faculties? or

- all programmes of a particular faculty such as arts, science, commerce, medicine, engineering, computers, technology, etc? or
- a combination of certain faculties?

(c) Whether a separate consortium is required for programmes offered in

- English medium only? or
- Hindi medium only?or
- Any one regicnal language (recognized language) only? or
- A particular group of languages only?

6. Which will be the body that will shoulder the responsibilities of formulating, establishing and coordinating activities of these consortia?

(a) Whether it should be a part of one of the distance education institutions or should it be totally an independent body, not under the control of any one of distance and open education institutions in any manner?

(b) Whether one of the distance and open education institutions should be assigned with the above responsibility or should it be the joint responsibility of all the distance and open education institutions as may be decided jointly by the Heads of the member institutions of consortium?

7. In case the consortium should be separate and independent body by itself whether it should have hierarchical structure in itself with coordinating bodies/ units at state and national level or there should be independent coordinating bodies for state consortia and a separate one for national consortium?
8. Whether there should be a common syllabus and standard quality course materials for any particular

programme(s) to be offered by the distance education institutions? If yes, what is the language in which the standard course materials are to be developed first? Should it be English or Hindi or both in the case of a national consortium? In case of State consortia should it be a regional language or any other language (recognized Indian Language)?

9. Whether it should be mandatory for the state level distance education consortia offering the same courses/ programmes in respective state language to use the translated version of the standardized course material, initially developed in English/Hindi medium at national level for national consortium?
10. Whether the comparison and establishment of parity or equivalence of course materials of different courses/ programmes of different distance education institutions is possible? If yes, what should be the agency and procedure to do it? Who should establish such agency and whether it would be acceptable to all distance and open education institutions?
11. Can a common course syllabus for the subjects on offer by different distance education institutions be developed? If yes, can the responsibility of course development for a particular course/programme be done on collaborative basis or should it be assigned to one particular institution so that all other distance education institutions can share the material?
12. What should be the structure and nature of student support services?

    (a) Whether there should be a separate structure for student support services for the consortium? Or should the existing support structures of different distance education institutions be pooled and treated as one for the purpose of providing support services to all students of the consortium?

    (b) Whether the institutions offering part-time contract services, as part of existing support structure of one

particular distance education institution, would agree to the above restructuring or pooling which puts additional pressure on their services?

13. What about the admission policy and procedures?

- Whether there should be a common policy and procedure for admission of students to all the institutions forming the consortium? or
- Whether each of these institutions should admit students as per their own policies which will be followed by consolidation, finalisation and preparation of common admission list?

14. What should be the timing and periodicity of examination for the students of member institutions of consortium?

- Whether common examination schedule, timings and periodicity for all the institutions of the consortium? Or
- Should there be different schedules, timings and periodicity for examinations of different institutions according to their convenience?

15. What should be the procedure for certification (award of certificates, degrees, diplomas, etc.) by the member institutions of consortium?

- Whether the institutions(s) where the student was initially admitted would do it? Or
- The institution under whose jurisdiction the student gives his/her final examinations should be doing it?.

Problems

Even if all the above issues are resolved there will still be some important practical problems connected to the issues of consortium. They can be as follows:

1. Identification of all programmes/courses offered by all the distance and open education institutions.
2. Classification of the programmes and courses into the following types.

   (*a*) programmes/courses offered by single mode institutions
   (*b*) programmes/courses offered by dual mode institutions
   (*c*) programmes/courses offered by discipline-wise or faculty-wise (Arts, Science, Commerce, Engineering and Technology, etc.)
   (*d*) Programmes/courses offered—according to medium of instruction (English, Hindi, Regional languages and in more than one language).

3. Pooling/collection of all the course materials of all the programmes offered by different distance and open education institutions.
4. Segregation of course materials of different programmes into basic/fundamental/core/compulsory courses and optional/applied/elective courses, wherever applicable.
5. Preparation of syllabus of various programmes/courses on offer.
6. Comparison, scrutiny and development of a common, acceptable and standarised syllabus and curriculum for each of the courses and programmes.
7. Comparison and scrutiny of the content of various courses and programmes of different institutions in the light of the standard syllabus and curriculum developed as above and establishment of parity and/or degree of variation among and between the courses/programmes accordingly.
8. Commission, omission, updating, etc. of the materials for development of standardised study materials for particular course/programme.
9. Quality testing, assessment and accreditation of all the specialised/new courses/programmes of

different institutions and their material with the purpose of accepting them as standard material for adoption by other institutions as they are or by translating them.

10. Identifying the regional institutions/universities that have potential for translating the standard material into the respective regional languages.
11. Establishing an appropriate mechanism for the purpose of monitoring the translation work of standard course material developed at national level into the respective regional languages by the regional institutions/universities.

All these issues and problems raised above are suggestive only, and not exhaustive. However, all these, amongst others, need to be thoroughly considered and addressed before evolving a meaningful and effective consortium or consortia for distance education in India. Once this happens it would be possible to reach out different kinds of hitherto unreached students through distance and open education on one hand and to reach the so called reached in an effective manner on the other.

Reference

Hornby, A.S. (Ed.), (1989). *Oxford Advanced Learner's Dictionary of Current English*, Fourth edition, Oxford: Oxford University press.

Longman (1985). *Longman Dictionary of the English Language*, Harlow: Longman Group Limited.

Pillai, C.R., and Naidu, C.G. (1997). *Economics of Distance Education: The IGNOU Experience*, Planning and Development Division, New Delhi: Indira Gandhi National Open University.

Terry Page G., J. B. Thomas, and A.R. Marshall (1979). *International Dictionary of Education*, London: The English Language Book Society and Kogan Page.

Webster, N. (1985). New Webster's *Dictionary of the English Language*, U.S.A.: Delair Publishing Company, Inc.

Index